MASTERING HIGH-STAKES TRANSITIONS

MASTERING HIGH-STAKES TRANSITIONS

TURNING DELAYS, SETBACKS, AND SILENCE INTO YOUR MOST STRATEGIC GROWTH

ROTIMI OWOADE

CHARIS & GRIT
BOOKS

Published by Charis & Grit Books

96 Durand Rd. Winnipeg MB. R2J 3T2 Canada

ISBN: 979-8-90417-212-1

Dedication

This book is dedicated to the memory of my beloved uncle, Oluremi Adeshina – a father like no other. The man who dared to dream and live his dreams by faith, and taught me to dream and live my dream by faith.

And to the One who orders my steps— Jesus Christ

PREFACE

Transitions often arrive unexpectedly. They can stem from job loss, stalled progress, failed projects, broken relationships, or long silences after a clear direction. For high-achieving leaders and professionals, these times can be especially jarring. The familiar signs of success vanish; titles provide no safety, skills don't always lead to progress, and effort often fails to yield quick results.

This book speaks to that uncertain space.

Mastering High-Stakes Transitions fills a void in leadership literature: a clear framework for handling interruptions, obscurity, and delays. While modern business culture celebrates growth—like promotions and visibility—it offers little guidance for setbacks. Yet history, psychology, and Scripture show that meaningful leadership often develops during challenging times, not during rapid growth.

At the heart of this book is a new understanding of transition. Drawing on Joseph's story and insights from neuroscience, leadership development, and organizational theory, it argues that delay is not an exception in leadership. Instead, it often builds capacity, integrity, and maturity. The pit, the house, and the prison aren't just hurdles; they are environments that prepare leaders for roles they might not otherwise manage.

This book is not about waiting passively or stagnating. It's about taking **active responsibility** when control is limited and outcomes are uncertain. The chapters explore how identity changes when roles shift, how integrity is tested when doing the right thing feels unrewarded, and how influence can grow without authority. Readers are encouraged to see silence not as abandonment, but as preparation—often hidden, often uncomfortable, but crucially important.

The approach is intentionally interdisciplinary. Scripture is treated with seriousness, not sentimentality. Psychological insights are used practically, not abstractly. Leadership theory serves as a tool, not an end goal. Throughout the book, relatable examples, reflective exercises, and actionable frameworks help readers move from confusion to clarity and from endurance to growth.

This book is for executives facing career disruptions, entrepreneurs recovering from failures, ministry leaders in obscurity, and professionals caught between what was and what lies ahead. It also appeals to those interested in faith-integrated leadership and values-driven business literature, seeking depth without oversimplification.

Mastering High-Stakes Transitions does not promise quick resolutions. Instead, it offers fresh perspectives. It provides language for understanding what difficult seasons produce beneath the surface and tools for engaging with intention. The goal is not just emergence, but sustainability—so that when opportunities arise, the leader who steps forward is ready not just to ascend, but to endure.

TABLE OF CONTENTS

INTRODUCTION

"When we are no longer able to change a situation, we are challenged to change ourselves."

— VIKTOR E. FRANKL

In the relentless rhythm of modern life, where success is measured in likes, launches, and quarterly reports, waiting feels like failure. We live in an era obsessed with acceleration. There are overnight sensations, viral breakthroughs, and instant gratification. The narrative screams: If you're not ascending, you're declining. If you're not visible, you're irrelevant. Yet, buried in the ancient story of a young dreamer named Joseph lies a counterintuitive truth: The most profound growth, the deepest character formation, and the greatest leadership potential are forged not in the spotlight of achievement, but in the shadows of obscurity. This book, ***Mastering High-Stakes Transitions***, is an invitation to reframe those hidden seasons—not as detours or dead ends, but as divine incubators designed to prepare you for a destiny you could never handle without them.

Consider Joseph's trajectory, as chronicled in Genesis 37-50. At seventeen, he was the favored son, cloaked in a coat of many colors. It was a symbol of paternal preference and prophetic promise. His dreams painted a future of supremacy, with stars and sheaves bowing before him. He was the archetype of potential: gifted, visionary, inevitable. But in a single, brutal afternoon, everything shattered. Betrayed by his brothers, stripped of his garment, and hurled into a dry cistern in the arid plains of Dothan, Joseph plummeted from heir to commodity. Sold for twenty shekels, the going rate for a slave in the Middle Bronze Age, he vanished into Egypt's underbelly, a nobody in a foreign empire. What followed was thirteen years of silence: slavery in Potiphar's house, false accusation, and imprisonment in a royal dungeon. No updates. No breakthroughs. Just the grind of obscurity.

If this were a modern LinkedIn bio, Joseph's profile would have flatlined. No promotions, no TED Talks, no viral posts. Yet, those "wasted" years were anything but. They were the crucible where arrogance was tempered into empathy, talent into wisdom, and dreams into deliverables. By the time Pharaoh summoned him, Joseph was unstoppable. He interpreted dreams, architected a national famine relief strategy, and rose to second in command of the world's superpower. His wait wasn't punishment; it was preparation. As Genesis 50:20 declares, "You intended to harm me, but God intended it for good to accomplish what is now being done, the saving of many lives."

This is the essence of ***Mastering High-Stakes Transitions***: recognizing that obscurity is not a tomb, but a womb. It's the darkroom where your leadership image develops, the gym where your character muscles are built. In a culture that pathologizes stillness, equating it with stagnation, we've lost the art of productive waiting. We scroll through feeds of curated success, internalizing the lie that if we're not "hustling" visibly, we're failing spiritually or professionally. But history, psychology, and Scripture converge on a different story. Great leaders aren't born on stages; they're forged in studios. Moses spent forty years in Midian's wilderness before leading Israel's exodus. David tended sheep in anonymity before slaying Goliath. Even Jesus waited thirty years in Nazareth's obscurity before His three-year ministry revolutionized the world.

Psychologically, this makes sense. Neuroscientists describe the "dopamine crash" that hits when external rewards—likes, promotions, applause—dry up. Accustomed to constant validation, our brains interpret silence as rejection, triggering anxiety or depression. Yet, this vacuum is fertile ground for what Erik Erikson called "identity formation." Stripped of titles and metrics, we're forced to confront the raw self: Who am I without the coat? This "identity quake," as explored in Chapter 1, shatters illusions of self-reliance, fostering radical dependency on God and intrinsic worth over performative value.

From a management perspective, obscurity aligns with proven frameworks like the Sigmoid Curve and Charles Handy's model of organizational lifecycles. Careers, like businesses, follow an S-shape: initial dip (learning), ascent (growth), plateau (maturity), and decline. To leap to a second curve or greater impact requires jumping during the plateau, often via a voluntary dip into the unknown. Joseph's pit was that dip: a forced reset that expanded his capacity from clan overseer to national savior. Modern leaders like Wayne (Chapter 1), demoted in a merger, or Sakura (Chapter 2), sidelined from worship leading, echo this. They pivoted from mourning lost status to mastering mundane tasks, emerging with deeper influence.

Mastering High-Stakes Transitions demands intentionality. It's not passive endurance but active stewardship. As John Maxwell's Law of the Process teaches, "Leaders develop daily, not in a day." Joseph didn't sulk; he served. In Potiphar's house, he managed logistics and personnel, honing skills for Egypt's granaries. In prison, he interpreted dreams for fellow inmates, networking with Pharaoh's cupbearer—a weak tie that unlocked his release. This is "active waiting": using delay to upskill, reframe narratives, and sow seeds of service.

Throughout this book, we'll dissect Joseph's anatomy of obscurity through a trilateral lens: biblical archaeology for historical grit, psychology for emotional insight, and management theory for practical strategy. Chapter 1, "The Anatomy of Obscurity," autopsies the pit's pain—social displacement, identity quake, spiritual silence—and reveals it as foundational digging for destiny's skyscraper. Chapter 2, "When Life Goes Silent," *dismantles the myth of linear growth, introducing the J-Curve: down to go up*. We'll explore Potiphar's paradox (success in slavery) and the integrity gap, where righteousness yields ruin yet builds resilience.

Deeper chapters unpack the prison's incubation: strategic networking (Chapter 3), deliberate practice (Chapter 4), and reframing failure as validated learning (Chapter 5). We'll draw on tools like Tony Robbins' neuro-associative conditioning to rewire victim mindsets into learner ones, and Peter Drucker's effective executive principles to manage up from the bottom. Modern illustrative stories—entrepreneurs navigating startup failures, executives surviving divorce—illustrate timeless truths.

By Chapter 10, "The Unstoppable Version of You," we'll synthesize emergence: stepping into visibility with maturity. You'll learn to override amygdala hijacks, leverage weak ties, and build sustainable systems. Each chapter ends with an "Obscurity Audit" or action guide: reflective prompts, reframing exercises, and servant steps to optimize your wait today.

This is theology in action. God wastes nothing. Your current silence, like a career stall, relational drought, spiritual vertigo, isn't abandonment; it's assignment. As Psalm 105:19 reflects on Joseph, "Until the time came to fulfill his dreams, the Lord tested Joseph's character." The test isn't to break you but to build you. The longer the wait, the more you can carry.

If you're in the pit, feeling invisible or betrayed, this book is your rope. If you're in prison, grinding without glory, it's your blueprint for a breakthrough. ***Mastering High-Stakes Transitions***, and watch obscurity birth opportunity. The palace doors aren't locked;

they're timed. Your emergence isn't if, it's when. Step into the hush. Do the work. The saving of many lives awaits.

AI tools were used in the creation of this book. The case studies used in this book are examples. Any similarities to actual persons are purely coincidental.

If you are navigating a high-stakes transition and want to apply this framework to your own situation with clarity and discipline, scan the QR code below for a Transition Readiness Chat.

CHAPTER 1

Obscurity as Formation: The Hidden Work That Stabilizes Leaders After the Sudden Stop

"There is no such thing as wasted time."
— Benjamin Franklin

The Sudden Stop

It happens in a heartbeat, often without a warning shot, a premonition, or a gentle deceleration. One moment, you are the protagonist of your own life, fully clothed in the coat of many colors—the visible, tangible signs of favor, success, and momentum. You are the "High Potential" employee earmarked for the C-suite, the visionary founder featured in industry journals as a "40 Under 40," or the worship leader whose voice moves the crowd and sets the spiritual temperature of the room. The sun is shining on your face, the wind is at your back, and the future looks like a straight, unbroken line of ascent. You feel inevitable. You feel protected by your own momentum. You believe the narrative that you are the author of your own ascent.

Then comes the pit.

For Joseph, the transition from the favored son of a patriarch to a piece of property in a Midianite slave caravan wasn't a gradual decline; it was a violent, jarring vertical drop. It was the sound of a tearing coat, the rush of adrenaline, the betrayal of blood, and the sudden, suffocating silence of a dry cistern. In a single afternoon, he went from the heir of the promise to a statistic in the ancient slave trade. He went from being the center of his father's world to being a commodity in a stranger's. The vertigo of this fall is not just situational; it is existential.

We call this place **Obscurity**.

In modern leadership culture, we are pathologically obsessed with the platform. We have monetized attention. We measure influence in followers, revenue, engagement metrics, and applause. We have conflated "being known" with "being significant." We live in an era of the "Personal Brand," where visibility is equated with viability. If it isn't posted, it didn't happen. If it isn't celebrated, it doesn't matter. Consequently, the anatomy of leadership is rarely studied in the dark, yet that is precisely where it is formed. We love the stage, but we fear the studio where the art is actually made.

Obscurity is the most terrifying, avoided, and misunderstood season in a leader's life. It is the desolate place where your external identity (like your title, your budget, your reputation, your access) is stripped away, leaving you with nothing but your raw character and your God. It is the "Unseen Curriculum" that no business school teaches, but every great leader must pass. It is the wilderness between the promise and the palace. It is the place where you are hidden *from* the world so you can be formed *for* the world.

Psychologically, this transition is traumatic. It triggers what neuroscientists call a "dopamine crash" or a "prediction error." The brain, accustomed to the constant reward loops of recognition, achievement, and social feedback, is suddenly starved of its usual chemical feedback. The silence is deafening. The lack of notifications feels like an indictment. We tend to view this withdrawal as a penalty box—a sign that we have failed, that our strategy was flawed, or that God has forgotten us. We interpret silence as rejection. We interpret the lack of movement as the death of the dream. We equate stillness with stagnation, forgetting that the most profound growth happens in the quiet.

But if we look through the trilateral lens of history, psychology, and spiritual formation, we see a different truth. Obscurity is not a tomb; it is a womb. It is the darkroom where the image of the leader is developed. It is the crushing floor where the olive yields its oil. Without the crushing, there is no anointing. There is no such thing as a "ready-made" leader; there are only leaders who have been forged in the fire of the hidden years. The duration of your obscurity often correlates with the magnitude of your destiny. The deeper the foundation needs to be, the longer you must stay in the hole digging.

This chapter is an autopsy of that season. We are going to dissect what happens emotionally, psychologically, spiritually, and socially when the lights go out. We will look at Joseph, not as a stained-glass figure frozen in stoic victory, but as a young man dealing with complex trauma, cultural displacement, and the crushing weight of invisibility. And we will walk alongside three modern leaders who found themselves in the same pit, examining their pain and their eventual pivots.

If you are currently in a season where you feel invisible, sidelined, or forgotten: **Welcome to the most critical work of your life.**

The Pain of Displacement

The Architecture of the Pit

To truly grasp the horror of Joseph's fall, we must understand the archaeology of the cistern. In the arid landscape of Dothan, these were not open, picturesque wishing wells. They were strictly utilitarian, bottle-shaped reservoirs carved deep into the limestone bedrock to capture rare flash floods. They featured narrow, restrictive necks that opened up into wide, bulbous bottoms.

Once thrown in, escape was physically impossible without external help. The walls sloped inward, slick with algae, mud, or limestone dust. It was dark, damp, and claustrophobic. When the biblical text notes the pit was "empty of water," it implies a place of death. Without water, in the Near East, there is no life. Joseph was placed in a literal architectural dead-end. He was suspended in the earth, cut off from the horizon, waiting to die. He could see a circle of sky, but he could not reach it. He could hear his brothers eating above him, oblivious to his terror.

This physical reality mirrors the social reality of the leader in obscurity: **You cannot climb out of this by yourself.** The very skills that got you up the mountain, like your vision, your charisma, your relentless drive, your ability to "make things happen," are useless against the smooth, indifferent walls of the pit. You are at the mercy of forces you cannot control, a terrifying prospect for any high performer used to dictating terms. This architecture forces a shift from self-reliance to radical dependency. It strips the leader of the illusion of control. It forces you to look up, because looking out is no longer an option.

The Law of the Vacuum

When Joseph was in Canaan, his identity was thoroughly reinforced by his social environment. He had the tunic—a distinct badge of rank that set him apart from his laboring brothers. He had the ear of the father—access to the supreme authority of the clan. He had the dreams—a divinely sanctioned narrative of future supremacy. His social standing provided him with a mirror that reflected a pleasant, coherent image: *You are special. You are chosen. You are the heir.*

Then, he is sold. He arrives in Egypt, and for the first time in his life, he is a nobody. He is a Hebrew (a derogatory outsider status) in a sophisticated Hamitic culture, a slave in a rigid stratocracy. He has no rights, no name recognition, and zero social capital. He has no past that anyone respects and no future that anyone acknowledges.

This is **Social Displacement**. It is the first and most jarring fracture in the anatomy of obscurity. It is the vacuum created when the external props of your identity are removed, and you are forced to confront the existential question: *Do I exist if no one acknowledges me?* In ancient sociology, this was akin to "Civil Death." You were physically alive but socially expunged. You become a non-person, an object of utility rather than a subject of dignity.

Consider **Wayne**.

Wayne was a high-performing director of operations at a Fortune 500 logistics firm. He was known as the "fixer." If a supply chain broke in rigid timelines, if a distribution center went offline, Wayne was the one they flew in on the corporate jet. His identity was inextricably tied to his calendar, which was always triple-booked, and his inbox, which was a constant stream of urgent, high-stakes decisions. He thrived on the adrenaline of being "The Guy." His cortisol levels were high, but so was his self-importance. He measured his worth by his exhaustion.

Then came the merger, a "strategic realignment" designed to trim redundancies and streamline operations. It was a sterile corporate term for a personal catastrophe.

Wayne wasn't fired. He was "retained." But his portfolio was absorbed by a new VP from the acquiring company, a woman ten years his junior with a different methodology and a mandate to modernize. Wayne was given a generic title, *special projects consultant*, and moved from a corner office with a view of the skyline to a shared workspace on a quiet, administrative floor.

The transition was brutal in its silence. The phone stopped ringing. The urgent emails stopped coming. The calendar, once a fortress of importance, was suddenly vast and empty. Wayne walked the hallways and felt like a ghost. People who used to stop and ask for his approval, who used to laugh too hard at his jokes, now nodded politely and kept walking, their eyes fixed on their next meeting—a meeting Wayne wasn't invited to. He felt a phantom limb sensation; he kept reaching for authority that was no longer there. He wasn't dead, but socially, he had ceased to exist in the hierarchy of importance. He had become organizational furniture. The "vacuum" sucked the air out of his self-worth. He found himself lingering in the coffee break room just to have a human interaction, only to realize he had nothing to talk about other than work that was no longer his.

The Org Chart Fallacy

Wayne fell victim to the **Org Chart Fallacy**: the pervasive belief that leadership is defined by lines, boxes, and reporting structures. Modern management theory distinguishes between *Formal Authority* (assigned power, budget control, hiring rights) and *Moral Authority* (earned influence, trust, respect). When the formal authority evaporates, the leader discovers how much moral authority they actually possess.

In the pit, Joseph lost his Formal Authority (the coat). He had no budget, no direct reports, and no freedom. But he began to build Moral Authority. He began to influence the environment through service rather than command. In a modern context, Wayne is being forced to shift from "Positional Leadership" (Level 1 in Maxwell's 5 Levels) to "Permission Leadership" (Level 2), where people follow him because they want to, not because they have to. This is the crucible of true influence. It transforms the leader from a "Boss" into a "Guide."

For any hope of fortune reversal, Wayne had to stop mourning the loss of his title and start leveraging his competence. The grief of the lost role was real, but it was becoming a barrier to his impact. He began to look outward. He noticed the younger analysts, overwhelmed by the merger and drowning in new protocols. He didn't have to help them; it wasn't in his job description. But he chose to. He began to mentor them, reviewing their reports, calming their anxieties, and teaching them the nuances of the business. He started serving without a title. He moved from being a "boss" who drives compliance to being a "leader" who cultivates potential. He realized that while his *scope* had diminished, his *impact* could actually deepen. He was no longer moving cargo; he was moving people.

If you feel invisible when you walk into a room, or find yourself checking your phone, hoping for a notification that proves you are needed, recognize this as a social symptom of displacement. You are suffering from "Status Anxiety." The required shift is to stop looking for recognition and start looking for a towel. Ask yourself: *Who can I serve today who can do nothing for me in return?* If you are invisible, you are in the perfect position to do the work that matters without the distraction of the applause.

The Identity Quake

The Household of Potiphar

Joseph enters the household of Potiphar, the "captain of the guard." We often imagine this as a simple domestic servant role, but historically, large Egyptian estates were complex micro-economies. They included granaries, cattle yards, bakeries, weaving shops, and extensive agricultural lands. The "steward" or "overseer" is the role Joseph eventually earned. It was essentially a **Chief Operating Officer (COO)** of a mid-sized conglomerate.

Joseph didn't just scrub floors; he learned logistics, supply chain management, resource allocation, and personnel oversight in a cross-cultural environment. He learned the Egyptian language, the court's codes, and the economics of the Nile. The "pit" of slavery was actually a high-level masterclass in Egyptian administration, the very skill set he would need to save the world from famine later. Providence was disguising a promotion as a demotion. He was being trained for a throne while wearing chains. He was learning to manage scarcity before he was asked to manage abundance. He was learning to serve an Egyptian master so he could one day lead the Egyptian nation.

Psychological Armor

Psychologically, obscurity triggers a crisis of the "Ideal Self." Tony Robbins talks about the "stories" we tell ourselves to make sense of our existence. We construct an identity—an avatar—that we present to the world to ensure our survival and status. We tell ourselves, "I am the provider," "I am the creative genius," "I am the visionary," or "I am the one who always wins." These stories become our psychological armor.

When Joseph was stripped of his coat, he was stripped of his avatar. He could no longer rely on the external validation of being the "dreamer." He had to find out who he was when the dream seemed dead. This leads to a psychological state known as **Identity Foreclosure Collapse**. We often commit to an identity too early. We might claim "I am a musician" or "I am a CEO." When that role is removed, we don't just lose a job; we lose the self. The neural pathways associate with that identity begin to degrade, causing genuine psychological distress, panic, and even depression. It is a form of grief. We mourn the person we used to be. The silence of obscurity forces us to confront the terrifying possibility that our value was purely instrumental.

Consider **Sakura**.

Sakura was a gifted worship leader, a prodigy who had been on stage since she was sixteen. For seven years, she defined the spiritual culture of her large church. Her voice was the soundtrack of the congregation's Sunday morning. She wrote the songs; she led the holy moments. Her identity was fused with her gift. The platform was her oxygen. She felt most alive, most connected to God, when the lights were on and the monitors were up.

Then came the pivot. The church leadership, anxious about aging demographics, decided they needed to reach a younger generation. They hired a twenty-two-year-old worship pastor with a raw, indie sound and a massive Instagram following. Sakura wasn't fired. She was "transitioned" to the choir. She was asked to "pour into the next generation," to mentor the new guy, to sing background vocals. It was framed as "discipleship," but it felt like replacement.

The first Sunday she stood in the back row, holding a microphone that was turned down in the mix, she experienced a psychological break. She watched the new guy sing *her* song, the one she wrote in a season of deep pain, and the crowd responded to him just as they had to her. It wasn't just jealousy; it was an identity quake. She felt erased. If she wasn't the voice leading the room, *who was she?* The silence of the background vocals felt like a judgment. She wondered if God had lifted His anointing from her. She felt like an heirloom. She was respected for the past, but irrelevant to the future.

The Lifecycle

In business strategy, the **Sigmoid Curve** explains the lifecycle of a product, an organization, or a career. There is a learning phase (the dip), a growth phase (the ascent), a maturity phase (the peak), and, inevitably, a decline. To survive, a business must jump to a *second curve* before the first one flatlines.

The tragedy is that most leaders hold on to the first curve too long because it feels safe. Sakura was clinging to her First Curve (The Performer). Obscurity was forcing her to jump to her Second Curve (The Mentor/Developer/Matriarch). The gap between the curves is always terrifying—it is a "liminal space" or a "valley of uncertainty." But that valley is the only path to longevity. If Sakura stayed on the first curve, she would become bitter and irrelevant. By jumping, she could become timeless. The First Curve is about *success* (what you achieve); the Second Curve is about *significance* (who you enable). The pain Sakura felt was the friction of the jump.

The Psychology of Detachment

Obscurity forces us to detach our *Who* from our *Do*. Ken Blanchard often reminds us, "God is more interested in your character than your comfort." In the psychological anatomy of obscurity, God is performing surgery on your ego. He is separating your soul from your role. This is known as breaking **Role Enmeshment**. When we are enmeshed, we bleed when our role is cut.

For Sakura, the pain of obscurity was actually the pain of an idol dying. She had made an idol of her own ministry. She needed the stage to feel loved by God. The "back row" was the only place she could learn that she was a daughter of God *before* she was a singer for God. The silence of the background vocals was where she heard the Father's voice most clearly. It was the only place she could learn that she was loved not for her melody, but for her heart. She realized she had been performing for approval rather than ministering from approval.

For a positive turnaround, Sakura had to reframe the narrative using **Cognitive Reframing**. She had to catch her automatic negative thoughts ("I am being replaced," "I am expiring") and replace them with truer, more empowering narratives. She needed to move from the **Scarcity Mindset**, which told her that there was only so much room at the table, to the **Abundance Mindset**, which revealed she was being replanted for a different kind of harvest. Her identity was not the spotlight; it was the light she carried. She was shifting from a performer to a matriarch, a role with less glory but far more legacy.

If you feel a deep sense of shame or worthlessness because your output has decreased, feeling like a "has-been" or experiencing withdrawal from the drug of "busyness," you are in the middle of the quake. The shift requires you to divorce your ego from your outcomes. Your worth is intrinsic, not performative. Repeat this truth until it settles in your bones: *I am not what I do. I am not what I have. I am not what people say about me.*

The Silence and the Sovereign

The Round House

When Joseph is thrown into prison after the false accusations of Potiphar's wife, the Hebrew text uses a rare, specific word: *Bet Sohar*, often translated "Round House" or "Fortress." This wasn't a common, rat-infested jail for thieves and murderers; it was the king's prison. It was a high-security holding tank for political prisoners and high-ranking officials who had fallen out of favor with Pharaoh, such as the Chief Cupbearer and the Chief Baker.

This detail changes everything. Joseph wasn't in the general population; he was in a white-collar detention center for the elite. Even in his deepest dungeon moment, God placed him in the one specific location where he could network with the king's inner circle. He was rubbing shoulders with the intelligentsia of Egypt. The archaeology reveals a strategic positioning even in suffering. God was placing Joseph in the waiting room of the palace. It was confinement, yes, but it was *strategic* confinement. He was in the only place where he could meet the one man (the cupbearer) who could eventually introduce him to Pharaoh.

The Dark Night of the Calling

The most terrifying part of Joseph's story is the timeline. We read Genesis 37 to 41 in ten minutes. Joseph lived it for *thirteen years.* Thirteen years is a lifetime for a young man. It is the prime of his youth, given to silence. It is a delay that screams denial.

- Thirteen years of waiting.
- Thirteen years of doing the right thing and getting the wrong result (refusing Potiphar's wife led to prison, not promotion).
- Thirteen years of helping others succeed (interpreting the cupbearer's dream) and being forgotten in return.

Spiritually, obscurity feels like abandonment. It is what St. John of the Cross called the "Dark Night of the Soul." It is the season where your theology doesn't seem to match your reality. *It is where you learn to trust the Hand of God even when you cannot trace the Heart of God.* It is the purification of motive. You learn to serve God for who He is, not for what He gives.

Consider **Anita**.

Anita was a firebrand entrepreneur. She felt a clear, undeniable calling to launch a faith-based tech startup. She raised capital, hired a passionate team, and prayed bold prayers. She believed this was her "Joseph moment"—her ascent to the palace to fund the Kingdom. She had the verses, the confirmation, and the drive. She had built the ark, but the rain never came.

Two years in, the market crashed. The venture capital dried up. The product failed to find a market fit. Anita had to do the hardest thing of her life: she had to fire her friends. She had to liquidate the assets. She had to shut down the servers—a digital death. Broke, humiliated, and broken, she moved back into her parents' basement at age thirty-two.

She sat in that basement, her personal cistern, surrounded by boxes of unsold merchandise, which felt like tombstones of her dream. She was spiritually shattered. She had stepped out in faith, and the water didn't part; it drowned her. She felt duped by God. She scrolled LinkedIn, watching her peers get promoted, get funded, and become successful, while she sat in the dark. She asked the question that haunts every leader in obscurity: "Why did you give me the vision if you were going to lead me to the pit?" She felt that God was a prankster, or worse, absent. She began to doubt not just her competence, but her calling. She wondered if she had hallucinated the voice of God.

The J-Curve and The Pivot

In private equity and startups, the **J-Curve** describes the tendency for an investment's performance to drop sharply immediately after launch due to capital costs, before it eventually rises to new heights. You have to "go down to go up."

Anita was in the dip of the J-Curve. Strategically, this is known as the "Valley of Death." But in Lean Startup methodology, this failure is not a verdict; it is **validated learning**. It is data. The failure of the first venture was necessary to teach her the resilience and market insight needed for the second. The first business wasn't the destination; it was the tuition.

God was using the wilderness to break her addiction to **Linear Progression**. We are culturally conditioned to think God leads in straight lines (Dream → Success). Joseph's life shows us God leads in spirals (Dream → Pit → Slavery → Prison → Palace). The path up is down. This is the **Theology of the Limp**. Just as Jacob wrestled with God and walked away with a limp, Anita needed to be wounded in her self-sufficiency so she could be healed in her dependency.

To step forward, Anita had to stop asking "Why?" and start asking "What?"

- *Not:* "Why did this happen to me?" (The Victim Mindset, which leads to bitterness and stagnation).
- *But:* "What are you trying to build in me that could not be built in a boardroom?" (The Learner Mindset, which leads to growth and perspective).

Anita began to rebuild a rhythm of grace. She took a lowly job to pay the bills. She paid off debts slowly, dollar by dollar. She learned humility. She learned that **Failure is an event, not a person.** When she launched her next venture five years later, she wasn't the brash, fragile founder she had been. She was a rock. She had a "limp," like Jacob, and that limp made her trustworthy. Investors backed her not because she was undefeated, but because she was unbreakable. She carried a weight of glory she could not have carried five years prior.

If you find you cannot pray because you are angry, or you feel God has broken His promise and are experiencing "spiritual vertigo," pause here. Trust the slow work of God. We overestimate what we can do in a year and underestimate what God can do in a decade. Embrace the silence as intimacy, not distance. The teacher is always silent during the test.

Leveraging the Pit

If you are in obscurity, you have a stark choice. You can decay, or you can develop. You can become bitter, or you can become better. The pit is neutral; your response determines the outcome. Many people go into the pit and die there. Others go into the pit and come out as princes. How do we practically navigate this anatomy? We apply the **Law of the Process**.

1. Master the Mundane

Joseph didn't sulk in Potiphar's house. He didn't perform the bare minimum. He worked, organized, and optimized. He brought order to chaos. He understood that **how you do anything is how you do everything.** He treated Potiphar's house as if it were his own, stewarding resources that didn't belong to him.

Action: If you have been reorganized out of a big role, become the absolute best at the small role. Bring excellence to the invisible tasks. If you are washing dishes, wash them like you are washing the feet of Jesus. Build a reputation for faithfulness in the small things. As John Maxwell says, "Small disciplines repeated with consistency every day lead to great achievements gained slowly over time." Excellence in the dark is the price of admission for influence in the light.

2. Maintain Your Integrity When No One is Watching

When Potiphar's wife tempted Joseph, no one would have known if he said yes. He was a slave; he had "needs," he was lonely, and his own family had betrayed him. He had every societal excuse to indulge. But Joseph knew that character is what you do in the dark. He knew that compromising his private world would eventually collapse his public world. He valued his connection with God more than his comfort.

Action: Use this season of obscurity to root out secret sins. Pornography, pride, financial looseness, hidden resentments—kill them now while the spotlight is off. If you can't handle the darkness, you will burn up in the spotlight. Integrity is a muscle that must be exercised when the resistance is highest. This is "Shadow Work" or confronting the dark parts of your own soul before you are given authority over others.

3. Serve Another Person's Dream

This is the hardest step. In prison, Joseph saw the cupbearer and baker looking dejected. He asked, "Why are your faces so sad today?" He had every right to be self-absorbed, but he chose empathy. He used his spiritual gift to interpret the cupbearer's dream, helping someone else get promoted back to the palace while he stayed behind in the dungeon.

Action: Find someone else to win. Mentor a younger leader. Promote a colleague. Connect two people who can help each other. The fastest way to get out of your own depression is to contribute to someone else's progression. Sow seeds in a field you may not harvest. This breaks the spirit of self-pity and activates the spirit of generosity. It proves to God that you can be trusted with the care of His people, not just the fulfillment of your dream.

The Launchpad

The story of Joseph ends in the palace, with the signet ring and the royal robe. But that is not the point of the story. The point is that the Joseph who entered the palace was not the same Joseph who left Canaan.

The Joseph of Canaan was talented, but he may have been arrogant. He was a favored son, but he wasn't a father to the nation. He had the vision, but he lacked the vessel to carry it. The pit was the pottery wheel where the vessel was shaped. The Joseph who came out of the pit was empathetic, wise, tempered, and broken in all the right places. He was ready to save the very brothers who betrayed him, not destroy them. He had learned that power is for service, not for status. He understood that his elevation was for the salvation of many lives, not the inflation of his own ego.

Obscurity is not the end of your story. It is the refining fire. It is the anatomy of your future greatness. It is the necessary prerequisite for carrying the weight of glory.

To the Wayne reading this, know that your influence is growing in the silence. You are redefining what leadership looks like. You are moving from a manager of tasks to a leader of people. Your greatest contribution is not on the org chart; it is in the hearts of those you are mentoring. To the Sakura reading this, your song is becoming deeper in the dark. You are finding a melody that will heal hearts because it comes from a healed wound. You are trading the applause of the crowd for the approval of the king, and your legacy will outlast your voice. To the Anita reading this, your foundation is being solidified in failure. You are building a kingdom, not just a company. You are learning that God is the provider, not the market. The next venture will stand because you knelt.

Do not despise the day of small beginnings. Do not curse the darkness. Light a candle. Do the work. Keep your heart pure. God knows where you are. He has your GPS coordinates. *And when the character matches the calling, the palace doors will open.* But until then, serve faithfully in the pit.

The Obscurity Audit

Part 1: Identify Your Pit Reflect on which form of obscurity you are facing right now. Be honest with your assessment.

- **Social Obscurity:** Loss of status, title, inclusion, or feeling "out of the loop."
- **Professional Obscurity:** Career setback, firing, stagnation, or the "Valley of Death" in business.
- **Spiritual Obscurity:** A sense of God's silence, a delayed promise, or a confusing season of waiting.

Part 2: We live in the feeling of our thinking. Change the meaning, change the life.

- Write down the disempowering meaning you have given this season (e.g., "This means I am a failure," "God has left me," "My best days are behind me").
  - *Your Thought:* ______________________________
- Write a new, empowering meaning based on God's truth (e.g., "This means God is preparing me for a weight of glory I cannot yet carry," "I am in training for reigning").
  - *Your Truth:* ______________________________

Part 3: Servant leadership starts with the heart. Identify one person in your sphere who needs help succeeding this week—someone who can do nothing for you.

- *Name:* ______________________________

- *Action:* I will help them by______________________

"You intended to harm me, but God intended it for good to accomplish what is now being done, the saving of many lives." — Genesis 50:20

If you are navigating a high-stakes transition and want to apply this framework to your own situation with clarity and discipline, scan the QR code below for a Transition Readiness Chat.

CHAPTER 2

The Descent Curve: Leading Through Sudden Loss and Identity Collapse

"The impediment to action advances action. What stands in the way becomes the way."

— Marcus Aurelius

Everything rises and falls on leadership, but no one tells you how fast the fall can be. We are conditioned by a modern corporate and spiritual culture that strictly worships the ascent. We are addicted to the "up and to the right" trajectory. We celebrate the launch, the IPO, the grand opening, and the viral moment. We have charts for quarter-over-quarter growth, metrics for scaling, and endless seminars on how to climb the ladder. But we have almost no curriculum for the descent. We have no syllabus for the crash.

In our cultural narrative, the hero's journey is always about conquering the mountain. But in the biblical narrative, the leader's formation almost always begins with surviving the valley. We confuse "Resume Virtues" (the skills we bring to the marketplace) with "Eulogy Virtues"—the character that sustains us when the market crashes.

One moment, Joseph is wearing the coat. It's the Ancient Near Eastern equivalent of the corner office, the verified checkmark, and the championship ring all rolled into one. He is the favored son, the dreamer, the visionary with the clear trajectory. He has the "Identity." He perceives his life as a straight arrow pointing toward inevitable greatness. He is young, he is gifted, and he is undeniably arrogant. He believes the dream is for his glory, rather than for God's utility. He thinks the sun, moon, and stars are bowing to *him*, rather than to the God *in* him. He has confused "Anointing" with "Approval."

The next moment? He is in a pit. And just when he thinks he has climbed out, he finds himself in the confusing paradox of **Potiphar's House**, a gilded cage of high-functioning exile.

There is no transition period. There is no severance package. There is no off-boarding process, no exit interview with HR, and no golden parachute. There is only the sudden, violent stripping of the coat, the sound of tearing fabric, and the terrifying thud of hitting the bottom of a dry cistern, followed by the disorienting grind of managing an estate that isn't yours.

The Myth of Linear Growth

This sudden vertical drop contradicts everything we are taught about success in the Western world. We believe in linear accumulation: you work hard, you get results, you get promoted, you get happy. We believe that if we do good, good will happen to us. We operate on a karmic assumption that righteousness guarantees an upward slope. We treat God like a vending machine: insert obedience, extract blessing.

But the Joseph narrative shatters the myth of linearity. It introduces us to the **"J-Curve"** of spiritual and leadership formation. The J-Curve posits that the path to the palace inevitably, and traumatically, loops downward through the prison before it can ever hook upward toward destiny. It warns us of the **False Summit**—the season in Potiphar's house where you are successful on paper but enslaved in reality. You are competent, you are entrusted with power, you are generating revenue, yet you are utterly misaligned with your destiny. You are a "successful slave." *This phase is often more confusing than the pit because the external metrics say you are winning, but your internal compass says you are lost.*

The descent is the prerequisite. *The depth of your future influence is directly proportional to the depth of your current valley.* You cannot build a skyscraper on a tent foundation; God has to dig down before He builds up.

It Wasn't Just a Jacket

Let's get real for a second and dismantle the Sunday School image of Joseph. We are often taught that Joseph wore a "technicolor dream coat," a garment of mere aesthetic beauty. We imagine it like a costume from a Broadway musical. But the Hebrew phrase *ketonet passim* suggests something far more significant: a long-sleeved tunic extending to the ankles, likely embroidered or woven with rare dyes that were labor-intensive to produce.

In the Bronze Age labor market, this was not party wear; it was political wear. Field workers, shepherds, and laborers wore short tunics for movement. They needed their limbs free for the hard labor of wrestling sheep, digging wells, and hauling grain. A long-sleeved tunic was the uniform of the overseer—the one who managed, not the one who toiled. The sleeves themselves were a statement: "I do not use my hands for labor; I use my mind for strategy."

When Jacob gave Joseph this coat, he was not just giving him a fatherly gift; he was giving him a rank. He was bypassing the primogeniture (the rights of the firstborn, Reuben) and installing Joseph as the strategic manager of the clan. The coat was a sign that Joseph was exempt from the manual labor his brothers endured under the hot Canaanite sun. While they sweated, he supervised. While they worked, he watched. To his brothers, the coat wasn't just beautiful; it was a daily, visual reminder of their displacement. It was a target on his back.

Therefore, when his brothers stripped him of it, this was a corporate coup. They weren't just taking his clothes; they were liquidating his position. They were stripping his authority. They were forcing him from the C-suite back to the shop floor, and then beneath the floor into the basement. They were physically removing the symbol of his "specialness." They were tearing up the contract of his superiority.

The Psychology of "The Strip"

In modern psychology, we call this phenomenon **"Identity Foreclosure."** It occurs when an individual's self-concept is too tightly bound to a specific role or external validation early in life. They don't just *do* the job; they *become* the job. This is often seen in child actors, prodigy athletes, and young executives who rise too fast.

When that role is removed, the person doesn't just feel sad; they feel they have ceased to exist. This is **"Role-Self Merger,"** where the boundary between the person and the position dissolves. The "Self" has no distinct shape without the container of the "Role." Without the "coat," Joseph wasn't just naked; he was a nobody. He had no internal definition of self that existed apart from his father's favor and his manager's tunic. He faced total identity disintegration.

This creates a collision between the **False Self** (the image we project to get love/success) and the **True Self** (who we are in God). The coat was Joseph's False Self—impressive, colorful, and commanding. The pit forced him to confront his True Self—vulnerable, frightened, and utterly dependent.

This is the first challenge of the Silent Season: **The Crisis of Relevance.** It forces you to answer the most terrifying question a leader can face: *Who are you when you are not generating results?* If you cannot answer that question, you are not ready for the Palace.

Consider **Michelle.**

For five years, Michelle built a lifestyle brand. She was the *ketonet passim* personified in the digital age. Every post was a dopamine hit of validation. Her engagement metrics were her heartbeat. She lived in the noise of constant feedback, checking her analytics the way a diabetic checks their insulin—it was a survival mechanism. Her worth was quantified, aggregated, and displayed publicly every single day. She lived in a hall of mirrors, and every like was a reflection that said, "You exist."

Then, the algorithm changed. Or perhaps, the culture shifted. Or maybe she just "aged out" of the demographic. Overnight, the engagement dropped. The comments section, once a roaring stadium of praise, went silent. Brands stopped emailing. The "blue checkmark" remained, but the influence evaporated. She tried to pivot—changing content styles, chasing trends, getting more vulnerable, posting more frequently—but the silence only deepened. She experienced **"The Phantom Vibration Syndrome"** of the soul—constantly checking for a notification that never came.

Michelle is Joseph in the *bor*. The "coat," her digital relevance, has been stripped. She is stuck in the bottleneck of obscurity, unable to climb out. She is staring at a screen that no longer loves her back.

Michelle isn't just dealing with a loss of income; she is dealing with a neurochemical crash. Her brain was wired for the noise of approval, conditioned to expect the serotonin and dopamine spikes that come from digital applause. The silence feels like death because, neurologically, it mimics the withdrawal symptoms of an addict. The silence is not just quiet; it is a state of withdrawal. The brain is screaming for the "hit" of validation. She asks the question

Joseph surely asked in the dark: *If I am not the favored manager, who am I? If I am not seen, do I exist?*

The Leadership Pivot: To begin this pivot, one must conduct a **Relevance Audit**. Write down the top three things that define your worth today, whether it be your title, net worth, follower count, or the success of your children. Be brutally honest. If any of these items depend on someone else's permission (like a boss, a spouse, or an audience) cross them out. What is left is your proper foundation. If the list is empty, that is okay; that is the starting point of the University of Obscurity. We build from zero, but this time, we build on rock.

The Dissonance of Disappointment (Potiphar's House)

The pit was traumatic, but Potiphar's house was a psychological labyrinth. Joseph is sold into slavery, but he does not die. Instead, he executes a massive "State Shift." He rises to become the CEO of Potiphar's estate. Genesis 39:2 tells us, *"The Lord was with Joseph, and he was a successful man."*

This section is critical because it represents the **False Summit**. Joseph has seemingly recovered. He is managing a massive Egyptian household, likely overseeing agricultural production, livestock, and domestic staff. But this success is a mirage. He is a "successful" slave. He has power, but no autonomy. He has authority, but no freedom. This is the **Paradox of High-Functioning Exile**.

Adaptive Leadership in a Hostile System

Scholar Nahum Sarna, in *Understanding Genesis*, points out the anomaly of a Hebrew slave attaining such rank in a xenophobic Egyptian society. This required **Adaptive Leadership** of the highest order. Joseph had to learn a complex language, master the economics of the Nile Delta, and navigate the delicate politics of an elite household. He practiced **"Antifragility."** He didn't just survive the disorder of being sold; he gained from it.

The text says Potiphar *"left all that he had in Joseph's charge, and because of him he had no concern about anything but the food he ate"* (Genesis 39:6). This is the pinnacle of delegation. Joseph was running the company. He was proving that his gift of administration was innate, not coat-dependent. He was proving that he could bless a pagan house just as easily as a covenant house. He was living out the **Potiphar Principle**: The environment prospers solely because of the leader's character.

The Integrity Gap: When Righteousness Invites Ruin

Then comes the test. It is not just a test of lust; it is a test of identity. Potiphar's wife does not just offer sex; she offers a shortcut to security. In the ancient world, aligning with the matriarch of the house was a *strategic power play*. To refuse her was not just sexual rejection; it was *political suicide.*

Joseph refuses. He names the sin against God and the betrayal against his master. He chooses the hard right over the easy wrong. He acts with absolute integrity.

And what is the result? He is falsely accused of attempted rape. He is stripped of his cloak (for the second time) and thrown into the royal prison.

This is the **"Integrity Gap."** It is the terrifying chasm between doing the right thing and getting the wrong result. Most leaders quit here. They say, "I played by the rules. I optimized the systems. I served the vision. I resisted temptation. And I still lost. God, this system is broken."

Robert Alter, in his literary analysis of Genesis, notes the irony: Joseph's garment is used as evidence *against* him. The symbol of his righteousness becomes the instrument of his condemnation. This dissonance is deafening. It screams that the universe is unjust.

Meet **Nico.**

Nico is a high-level executive. He is disciplined, a good provider, and a church elder. He viewed his marriage like a contract, similar to the ones he negotiates at work: *I provide security, fidelity, and resources; we stay together.* He optimized the marriage like a business unit. He was faithful. He was present. He did the "right things." He operated under the assumption that righteousness guarantees ROI (Return on Investment). He believed in a **"Transactional God"**—if I do X, God is obligated to do Y.

Nico is Joseph in Potiphar's house. He is the **Steward of a Failing Estate**. He is managing the household finances, the kids' schedules, and the emotional climate with executive precision, even as the intimacy withers. He is successful on paper (the bills are paid, the vacations are taken), but he is enslaved to a dynamic where he is not truly seen.

Then, the accusation comes. Maybe it's not a false rape charge, but it's a narrative revision. His wife leaves, citing "emotional neglect" or a "need for space," painting Nico as the villain in her story to justify her departure. Nico, who refused to cheat, who refused to check out, is now the bad guy.

Nico is left in the deafening quiet of a four-bedroom house. The silence is physical. He walks into the kitchen, and the lack of noise hits him like a physical blow. He falls into the **"Sunk Cost Fallacy"**, replaying the years invested and feeling robbed. The silence of the empty house shatters his strategic worldview. He feels invisible, rejected, and unjustly punished.

The Emotional Impact: Betrayal of Competence

Nico feels the **Betrayal of Competence**. He was good at being a husband, just as Joseph was good at being a manager, yet both ended up in solitary. The silence mocks his competence. It says, "Your goodness did not save you." He wrestles with the theological crisis: Is God good, or is He just absent? He feels he is being punished for his obedience.

From Transaction to Transformation, Ken Blanchard teaches us that the greatest leadership tool is perspective. In this moment, Nico has to move from a *transactional* relationship with God to a *transformational* one.

A transactional leader asks, "What do I get for my service?" A transformational leader asks, "Who am I becoming through this service?" Joseph didn't scream at the walls of the prison forever. He eventually looked around and asked, "Who needs help in here?" Similarly, Nico's healing begins when he stops trying to analyze the fairness of the trial and starts managing the ministry of the moment. He stops asking "Why is this happening to me?" and starts asking "What is this teaching me?" He realizes that his integrity wasn't a currency to buy a specific outcome; it was the foundation of his character, regardless of the outcome. He learns that God is not a merchant; He is a Maker.

To navigate this, one must adopt the **Twenty-Four-Hour Grief Rule**. Give yourself permission to grieve the loss of the "deal" you thought you had. Scream, cry, journal, or punch a pillow. But set a timer. When the timer goes off, you must ask: *What is my assignment in this prison?* You cannot lead if you are stuck in the victim state. Your pain is valid, but your assignment is vital.

The Paralysis of Invisibility

Joseph spent years in prison. Psalm 105:18 says, *"They bruised his feet with shackles, his neck was put in irons."* The Hebrew implies something even more visceral: "His soul entered into the iron." The hardness of his environment began to test the softness of his spirit. The iron didn't just hold him; it defined his reality.

For a man of action, physical restriction is the ultimate torture. Joseph was a manager, an organizer, a grower. He was a man of "go." Now, his radius of influence is limited to a dungeon. He is in the **"Holding Pattern,"** the most dangerous phase of leadership development because it mimics death. It feels like a pause, but it is actually a crucible. It is the "Wait" that kills the will, or clarifies it.

This is the **Dark Night of the Soul**, where the sensory consolations of faith (the feelings of God's presence) are withdrawn to purify the will.

Think of **Davina**

She is a track star. Her body is her instrument. Her discipline is her worship. Her identity is speed. She speaks the language of split seconds and lactic acid. She has spent fifteen years optimizing her physiology for one specific output. She measures her worth in milliseconds. She has sacrificed social life, diet, and comfort for the god of Velocity.

One misstep. A torn ACL. A botched recovery. A complication during surgery.

Suddenly, the stadium lights are off. The team moves on. The coaches stop calling. She is dealing with **"Injury-Induced Obscurity."** She is in the dungeon. Her body, once her greatest asset, is now her prison cell. She can feel her muscles atrophying, and with them, her sense of self. The atrophy of muscle feels like the atrophy of her soul. She wakes up, and her first thought is not "What can I achieve?" but "What can I not do?"

Davina feels betrayed by her own vessel. She feels the "Silence of Capability." In psychology, we talk about the **Locus of Control**.

A person with an **External Locus** feels victimized by the injury, believing they cannot be happy until the external circumstance changes. They wait for the prison door to open, passive recipients of their fate. This leads to **Learned Helplessness**, the belief that no action matters, so why try? They become the "victim" of the narrative.

Conversely, a person with an **Internal Locus** realizes that while they cannot run, they still control their attitude, their rehab, and how they mentor the younger runners. They realize the prison is also a room to lead in. They shift from asking "When will I get out?" to "How do I lead while I am in?" This is **Learned Optimism**. It is the decision to find agency in the absence of autonomy. It is **Active Waiting** rather than Passive Waiting.

The Maxwell Law of the Lid

Joseph's "lid" was the prison bars. Davina's "lid" is her injury. But John Maxwell teaches that leadership ability is the lid that determines a person's level of effectiveness.

Joseph raised his lid *inside* the prison. When he couldn't manage Potiphar's estate anymore, he managed the prisoners' morale. He interpreted dreams. He checked on the baker and the cupbearer. He didn't wait for a position to practice his intuition. He didn't say, "I'll start interpreting dreams when I get my consultant fee." He gave his gift away for free in the dark. He practiced his future while still in his chains. He served his way into influence.

Davina must realize that her leadership was never about running; running was just the vehicle. Her discipline, her focus, her ability to overcome pain, those are transferable skills. She must shift her mindset from "I am a runner" to "I am a master of resilience."

In the silence of the rehab room, Davina is learning a level of mental toughness that the track could never teach her. She is learning to lead herself when no one is clapping. This is the hardest leadership of all: self-leadership in the dark. It is the training ground for the "Inner Game."

She begins a **Transferable Skills Inventory**. She lists the traits that made her successful in her previous season, such as discipline, vision, empathy, and strategic planning. Then, she identifies three ways those traits can be applied in her current season of limitation. If she can't run, perhaps she can write. If she can't manage a company, perhaps she can mentor a teenager. She finds a new outlet for the same voltage. The delivery mechanism has changed, but the power remains.

The Strategy of the Holding Pattern

Why does God allow the silence? Why does the text in Genesis span so many years of nothingness? Why does Joseph languish for two full years *after* interpreting the cupbearer's dream? From a strategic management perspective, the prison was not a pause; it was a pivot. It was an incubator for complexity. It was a holding pattern designed to broaden his runway.

1. The Silence Purifies Motives (The Stockdale Paradox): In the beginning, Joseph shared his dream with arrogance. "My sheaf stood up, yours bowed down." It was true, but it was self-aggrandizing. It was "I-centric." He used his gift to dominate his brothers, lacking emotional intelligence and awareness of the **Shadow Side of the Dream**. That great destiny requires great crushing. By the end, he had mastered what Jim Collins calls the **Stockdale Paradox**: You must retain faith that you will prevail in the end, regardless of the difficulties, and at the same time confront the most brutal facts of your current reality.

Joseph confronted the brutal fact of prison—the stench, the despair, the injustice, the rats—without losing the faith of the palace. He didn't succumb to toxic positivity nor to abject despair. He held the tension. This dual state of mind is the hallmark of **Level 5 Leaders**. The silence burns off the dross of ego, moving you from "I want to be great" to "I want to be useful," from ambition to assignment. It teaches you that the dream is not about your elevation, but about others' salvation.

2. The Silence Expands Capacity (Systemic Awareness): You cannot handle the weight of the Palace if you haven't built the muscle in the Prison. Consider the networking. Who was in that prison? The King's cupbearer and baker. These were high-level cabinet officials, the guys with the security clearance who knew the protocols of the throne room, who to bribe, who to trust, and how the bureaucracy of Egypt functioned.

In the dungeon, Joseph was getting a masterclass in Egyptian politics, court intrigue, and diplomacy from the very men who served Pharaoh. He listened to their stories. He learned the protocols of the court. He learned what made Pharaoh laugh and what made him angry. He wasn't just doing time; he was gathering **Systemic Awareness**. He was learning **Soft Power** influence without authority. God was giving him an MBA in Egyptian Governance while he sat in chains. If he had gone straight from the pit to the palace, he would have been culturally illiterate. The prison was his classroom.

3. The Silence Prepares You for the "Suddenly": Genesis 41:14 states, *"So Pharaoh sent for Joseph, and he was quickly brought from the dungeon."* When the silence breaks, it breaks fast. The Hebrew text suggests a rushed, chaotic transition. He had to shave, change, and stand before the most powerful man on earth in a matter of hours.

If you haven't used the silent years to prepare, you will be crushed by the sudden opportunity. This is the **Icarus Syndrome**—flying too high, too fast, on wax wings that melt in the sun. If Joseph had spent his prison years sulking, he would have been bitter, unkempt, and incoherent before Pharaoh. Instead, he was ready. He spoke with authority. He had a plan (the 20% tax reserve). He was ready to govern immediately.

The divorced professional creates a new, deeper life, and suddenly meets someone who values that depth, ready for intimacy because they have mastered solitude. The influencer builds a business based on value, not vanity, and suddenly finds sustainable success that isn't dependent on an algorithm. The athlete becomes a coach or a mentor, and suddenly influences thousands more than they ever did on the track.

A Practical Guide to Surviving the Silence

We don't just want to survive the silence; we want to leverage it. We want to graduate from the University of Obscurity with honors. Here is your battle plan, drawing on the best of leadership and spiritual psychology.

1. Reframe the Narrative

The quality of your life is the quality of your communication with yourself. Stop telling yourself the victim story that you have been demoted, dumped, or injured and that your life is over. That story creates a physiology of defeat; it slumps your shoulders and lowers your testosterone.

Instead, adopt the new story that you are in training. You are in the darkroom where the image is being developed. The darker the room, the clearer the picture. The heat of the fire is not to burn you, but to temper the steel. Every morning, thank God for the *training*, even if you hate the *circumstances*. Ask, "What muscle is being torn so it can grow today?" Treat your obscurity as a stealth mode for development. Visualize your future "Palace" moment not as a fantasy, but as a scheduled appointment you are preparing for. Use "incantations" or positive affirmations to rewire your brain's expectation of the future, telling yourself, "I am not rejected; I am redirected. I am not buried; I am planted."

2. Serve the Person in Front of You

When you are in the pit, you tend to become self-absorbed. Pain makes us narcissistic. We look inward and obsess over our own wounds. The way out is service. Joseph noticed that the cupbearer and the baker looked sad. In the middle of his own hell, he cared about their bad day. This is the ultimate servant leadership. It is counterintuitive to give when you are depleted, but it is the only way to tap into a new energy source.

Find one person today who is worse off than you and serve them. It breaks the cycle of self-pity. If you are unemployed, help someone fix their resume. If you are heartbroken, listen to someone else's story. If you are injured, encourage a healthy teammate. Service is the rope that pulls you out of the mental pit. It re-establishes your agency and your dignity. It triggers the **"Helper's High"** or a release of endorphins and oxytocin that combats the depression of the pit.

3. Lead Up

You don't need a title to lead. Joseph led in Potiphar's house, and he led in the prison. Influence is a choice, not a position. If you wait for the title to lead, you are not a leader; you are a bureaucrat. Real leaders lead when they have no authority to compel obedience. They lead through moral authority and competence.

Identify the "Pharaoh" or "Jailer" of your current limited environment (whether it is your physical therapist, your interim boss, or your children) and find a way to make their life easier today. Lead from the back of the line. Be the most useful person in the room, even if you are the lowest-ranked. Make yourself indispensable in the dungeon, and you will eventually be invited to the palace. Leadership is about adding value, not asserting authority.

My Thoughts

My friend, I do not know what pit you are currently standing in. I do not know how deep the silence is. I do not know how long you have been waiting for the rope to drop. I know the nights are long. I know the "Divorce Decree" feels like a failing grade on your permanent record. I know the silence of the phone not ringing feels like a rejection of your very soul. I know the injury feels like a theft of your destiny. I know the layoff feels like a judgment on your worth.

But look at Joseph. He was stripped of a coat, but he was robed in character. He was thrown into a pit, but he climbed out with a vision. He was silenced by his brothers, but he was given a voice that saved a nation. The very things that were meant to destroy him became the raw materials for his destiny.

You are not buried; you are planted. The silence is not the end of your story; it is the inhale before the shout of victory. Do not let the bitterness take root. Keep your heart soft. Keep your vision clear. Keep your hands busy serving. Do not waste the silence. Learn the lessons here that you cannot learn in the palace.

Your palace is coming. The question is, will you be the person of character who can inhabit it? Will you be ready to interpret the dream when the call finally comes? Or will you be so deafened by your own self-pity that you miss the knock at the door?

Wake up. Suit up. Show up. Even in the silence. Especially in the silence. Your time is now.

Reflect

Consider the "coat" that has recently been stripped from you. Was it a specific status, a role like the "perfect mom," or an identity like "the athlete"? Reflect on how much of your identity was wrapped up in that external validation. Next, look around your current "prison." Who is the "cupbearer" or "baker" in your life—someone suffering near you whom you can serve, despite your own pain? Who needs you to interpret their dream right now? Finally, examine the narrative you tell yourself. Write down the sentence you have been using to describe your current season (e.g., "I am a failure") and rewrite it using the lens of "Preparation" rather than "Punishment" (e.g., "I am in the conditioning phase for a heavier weight").

The "Silent Season" Twenty-One-Day Challenge

For the next twenty-one days, commit to the **"No Complaint, All Contribution"** challenge. First, you cannot verbalize a complaint about your situation to anyone but God in prayer; no venting to friends and no vague-booking on social media. Second, every day you must perform one act of anonymous service for someone in your "prison," be it your workplace, home, or community. Third, journal one thing you learned about your own character each night to track the shift in your internal locus of control.

If you are navigating a high-stakes transition and want to apply this framework to your own situation with clarity and discipline, scan the QR code below for a Transition Readiness Chat.

CHAPTER 3

Adaptive Leadership in Transition: Turning Obscurity into Capability

"It isn't the changes that do you in; it's the transitions."

— William Bridges

The Classroom You Didn't Choose

If you are reading this, you are likely standing in the hallway. You have left the room of "Known Success," where your identity was secure, your skills were celebrated, and your path was clear, and you have not yet entered the room of "Future Destiny." You are in transition. The wait. The grind. The season where the phone stops ringing, the accolades dry up, and the skills that once defined you seem suddenly irrelevant in a new, harsher context.

Psychologists and anthropologists describe this state as **liminality**, derived from the Latin word *limen*, meaning "threshold." Liminality is not merely a pause; it is a profound state of disorientation that occurs during rites of passage. It is the neurological no-man's-land where the initiate is stripped of their pre-ritual status but has not yet been inducted into their new standing. In this space, the old social hierarchies dissolve, and the future hierarchy has not yet formed. It is a terrifying, foggy vulnerability where the ego fights for survival because it has lost its usual markers of validation. St. John of the Cross called this the "Dark Night of the Soul"—a spiritual desolation that strips away our dependence on emotional highs to deepen our dependence on God. It is a purification of the will, a stripping of the spiritual ego that seeks God for His benefits rather than His presence.

The Architecture of the Wait

We often view waiting as "dead time" or a void to be filled with distraction until the "real life" resumes. However, developmentally, the wait is not empty; it is pregnant. It is an active state of incubation. Just as a seed must undergo the dark, crushing pressure of the soil to shed its hull and germinate, a leader must undergo the pressure of obscurity to shed the hull of the "False Self." We might call this **Spiritual Wintering**. In nature, winter is not death; it is a time of deep root development and resource conservation. Trees pull their sap down into their roots to survive the frost. Similarly, hard seasons force leaders to pull their identity down from the "leaves" of public performance into the "roots" of private character.

The Myth of Linear Progression

In modern leadership theory, we are obsessed with the "hockey stick" growth curve—the moment of rapid, exponential ascent. We consume biographies of titans that condense decades of struggle into a few breezy chapters before getting to the "good part." We rarely discuss the long, excruciating flat line that precedes the spike. We celebrate the breakthrough but ignore the breakdown that made it possible. We want the resurrection without the crucifixion.

This cultural obsession creates a false expectation of linear progression. We believe that if we work hard and pray hard, our influence should grow up and to the right, quarter over quarter. But the Kingdom trajectory is rarely linear; it is cyclical and often paradoxical. It involves descent before ascent. It requires a death of the false self before the birth of the true leader. It mirrors the growth of the Chinese Bamboo tree, which spends five years building a root system underground with no visible growth, only to shoot up eighty feet in six weeks. The obscurity *is* the growth. The silence *is* the sermon.

Tony Robbins, a master of peak performance psychology, often says, *"Life is not happening to you; it is happening for you."* That is a difficult pill to swallow when you are sitting in the ashes of a failed venture, navigating a career demotion that feels like a public shaming, or staring at the ceiling of a prison cell—whether that prison is made of iron bars, crippling debt, or professional irrelevance. But if we shift our state, if we consciously intervene in our physiology and our focus, we realize that this season of obscurity is not a burial. It is a planting.

This chapter explores the **Hidden Curriculum of Hard Seasons**. It is a curriculum that cannot be learned in a corner office, a celebrated pulpit, or an Ivy League classroom. It is the specific, rigorous, and often painful coursework designed to rewire your brain for resilience, expand your capacity for servant leadership, and solidify your character so that when—not if—you are elevated, you do not crush the people beneath you under the weight of your own insecurity.

We will look through the lens of one of history's greatest and most tested leaders: Joseph. We will go beyond the Sunday School summary and excavate the archeological realities of the Egyptian slave trade, the management principles of an ancient Major-Domo managing a complex household economy, and the neuroscience of trauma resilience. We will see how Joseph moved from the arrogance of a dreamer to the wisdom of a savior.

This is your invitation to stop wasting your pain. It's time to enroll in the curriculum.

The Neuroscience of the Pit

Reframing Trauma as Training

When Joseph was stripped of his coat of many colors, the symbol of his father's favor and his own identity, and thrown into a pit by his brothers, his brain likely entered a state of acute hyperarousal. The amygdala, the brain's threat detection center, would have been firing uncontrollably, hijacking his prefrontal cortex and flooding his system with cortisol and adrenaline.

When trust is broken by those closest to us (brothers, business partners, mentors), the brain processes it similarly to physical pain. Neuroimaging studies have shown that social rejection activates the **dorsal anterior cingulate cortex**, the same region that lights up during physical injury. It is a "fight, flight, or freeze" moment that often leaves deep psychological scarring. For Joseph, the shock was total. He went from being the princeling of the camp to a commodity in a hole. His HPA axis (hypothalamic-pituitary-adrenal axis) was stuck in the "on" position, a state that, if prolonged, leads to toxic stress and breakdown. He was experiencing what trauma experts call "moral injury"—a violation of his fundamental understanding of right and wrong by trusted authority figures.

To understand the terror, we must understand the setting. The "pit" mentioned in Genesis 37 was likely a water cistern carved into the limestone bedrock near Dothan. As previously stated, these were bottle-shaped—narrow at the top, wide at the bottom—making escape impossible without a rope. Dothan was not a quiet pasture; it was situated on the **Via Maris** (Way of the Sea), a major international trade route connecting the spice-rich regions of Gilead to the markets of Egypt. Joseph wasn't just thrown into a hole in the ground; he was thrown into the intersection of global commerce.

When he was sold to the Ishmaelites for twenty shekels of silver (the standard price for a slave in the Hammurabi era, confirming the historical accuracy of the text), he was forcibly transferred from a pastoral, tribal economy (shepherding) to a complex, international mercantile economy (the spice and slave trade). The text notes the traders were carrying "gum, balm, and myrrh." There is a cruel irony here: these were healing agents and perfumes destined for Egyptian embalming rituals, yet they were transporting a young man whose life was effectively being embalmed in slavery. The sensory overload, foreign languages, strange smells, the harsh discipline of the caravan, marked the beginning of his re-education. He was moving from a culture of verbal tradition to a culture of written record, from a culture of tents to a culture of stone.

The Science of Adaptive Capacity

Neuroplasticity is the brain's extraordinary ability to reorganize itself by forming new neural connections throughout life. For decades, scientists believed the brain was fixed after childhood. We now know that under conditions of high demand (specifically, the demand to survive and adapt to new, complex environments) the brain becomes incredibly plastic.

Research published in the *Journal of Personality and Social Psychology* suggests that "adversarial growth" or "post-traumatic growth" occurs when individuals are forced to accommodate new information that shatters their previous worldviews. For Joseph, the worldview that "I am the favored son, and the world revolves around me" was shattered in an instant. He had to build a new cognitive framework: "I am a survivor in a foreign land, and I must learn to add value to survive."

This cognitive restructuring is painful. It requires the biological "pruning" of old neural pathways associated with pride, entitlement, and reliance on family status. Simultaneously, it demands the forging and myelination of new pathways associated with situational awareness, emotional intelligence, and cross-cultural communication. Joseph had to learn Egyptian—not just the language, but the subtle, unwritten codes of conduct in a stratified society. He had to learn to read the room when he used to *be* the room. He had to develop **Cognitive Flexibility**, the mental ability to switch between thinking about two different concepts, and to think about multiple concepts simultaneously. He had to hold the reality of his slavery in one hand and the reality of God's presence in the other without letting the former negate the latter.

The Executive in the Trenches

Consider **Jon**.

For fifteen years, Jon was the VP of Operations for a mid-sized logistics firm. He had an executive assistant who managed his calendar, a corner office with a view of the skyline, and a team of forty people who jumped when he cleared his throat. He was a "Level 4 Leader" by Maxwell's definition—people followed him because of what he had done for the organization. He lived in the echo chamber of his own success.

Then, the merger happened. The efficiency consultants came in. The "redundancies" were announced. Jon was out.

After six months of deafening silence from recruiters and a shrinking severance account, Jon swallowed his pride and took a consulting gig for a chaotic startup run by a twenty-six-year-old founder. There was no assistant. There was no office—just a Slack channel, a shared desk in a noisy co-working space, and a laptop. His first task? To manually audit thousands of lines of shipping data—grunt work he hadn't touched since he was an intern in the late 90s.

Jon's initial reaction was a "State of Suffering." His physiology was slumped, his breathing shallow. His focus was entirely on the loss—the lost status, the lost income, the lost identity. His internal language was toxic, constantly repeating, *"I am better than this. This is beneath me. Do they know who I used to be?"* Psychologically, he was suffering from **Identity Foreclosure**. He had so tightly bound his self-worth to his title that the loss of the title felt like a loss of the self. He was grieving a death. He felt invisible, and for a leader used to visibility, invisibility is a form of torture. He found himself hesitating to introduce himself at parties because he didn't know how to answer the question, "What do you do?"

If Jon stays in this state, he dies professionally. His bitterness will seep into his work, and he will be fired. But Jon decides to engage the "Joseph Protocol." He changes his state. He stands up. He breathes. He realizes that for fifteen years, he had been leading from a spreadsheet, dangerously detached from the actual work.

He begins to see the manual data entry not as a punishment, but as a **re-skilling bootcamp**. As he sifts through the raw data, he spots patterns and inefficiencies that the high-level algorithms missed. He starts talking to the delivery drivers—the people he used to ignore in his previous role—asking them about their routes, their frustrations, their reality. He discovers that the "efficiency" metrics he used to enforce were actually causing bottlenecks on the ground because they didn't account for urban traffic patterns or loading dock delays.

Jon is rebuilding his dopamine reward pathways. Instead of getting dopamine from status (the title, the praise), he starts getting it from mastery (the work itself). He is relearning the nuts and bolts of his industry from the ground up. His brain is becoming more agile, shedding the rigidity of "executive privilege" for the flexibility of "startup hustle." He is developing **cognitive flexibility**. He is learning to speak the language of the coder and the driver simultaneously.

Six months later, Jon doesn't just present a report; he redesigns the startup's entire supply chain, saving them 30% in OPEX. He didn't outsource the solution; he *was* the solution. He regained his "moral authority" because he had returned to the trenches. He gained the young team's respect not because of his past title, but because of his current contributions. He realized that his previous title was a lagging indicator of past success, but his current work was a leading indicator of future value.

The Potiphar Principle

Servant Leadership When No One Is Watching

"The Lord was with Joseph, and he became a successful man, and he was in the house of his Egyptian master." — Genesis 39:2

Note the striking juxtaposition in the text: He was a slave, property of another man, yet the scripture calls him a "successful man."

In our modern Western lexicon, success is synonymous with autonomy. To be successful is to be your own boss, to call the shots, to have financial independence. In the Kingdom lexicon, success is synonymous with stewardship. Joseph in Potiphar's house is the ultimate case study in **Ken Blanchard's Servant Leadership,** combined with ancient **Household Management Theory**.

Potiphar is described as the "captain of the guard." In the Middle Kingdom period of Egypt, this title (*sar hat-tabachim*) likely meant he was the Chief of the Executioners or the head of the royal bodyguard. He was a high-ranking securocrat, intimately connected to the Pharaonic court. His estate would not have been a simple home; it was a complex micro-economy. It would have included granaries, weaving workshops, cattle herds, fields, and a retinue of scribes and laborers.

For Joseph to be appointed "overseer" (*paqid*) meant he wasn't just cleaning floors or serving wine. He was the CEO of a multimillion dollar enterprise. His management portfolio was vast.

First, he managed complex supply chains, sourcing food, linen, and materials for a noble house in a pre-industrial economy. He had to negotiate with local farmers and merchants to ensure the estate was stocked before the Nile floods receded. Second, he directed human capital, managing hundreds of other slaves and servants, navigating the complex hierarchy of Egyptian society where he was an outsider. He had to resolve disputes between servants and ensure productivity without the power of the whip, but rather through organization. This is remarkable because Joseph was a Hebrew, and Genesis 43:32 tells us that "Egyptians could not eat with Hebrews, for that is an abomination to the Egyptians." Joseph overcame deep-seated cultural prejudice through sheer competence, mastering the art of **Code-Switching** to adapt his behavior to Egyptian expectations. Finally, he was accountable for the financials. Ancient Egyptian estate managers had to account for every sack of grain and jar of oil to avoid theft accusations. The archaeological record is full of papyri from estate managers detailing these intricate inventories. Joseph learned double-entry bookkeeping before it was invented, learning the economics of scarcity and surplus on a micro-scale, which would later save the world on a macro-scale.

The Law of the Picture & Managing Up

John Maxwell's **Law of the Picture** states: *People do what people see.* Joseph's work ethic in Potiphar's house was not transactional (working for a paycheck); it was transformational (working to become a certain type of person). He led by example. He didn't wait for instructions; he anticipated needs.

But Joseph also mastered the delicate art of **Managing Up**. In a high-stakes environment where one mistake could mean execution (Potiphar was, after all, the executioner), Joseph built **Radical Trust**. This wasn't just about doing a good job; it was about creating **Psychological Safety** for his master.

Blanchard teaches that *"Servant leadership is all about making the goals clear and then rolling your sleeves up and doing whatever it takes to help people win."* Joseph made Potiphar "win" by removing all friction from his domestic life. He anticipated needs before they were spoken.

The Trust Vacuum: This highlights the crucial distinction between "delegation" and "abdication." Potiphar didn't just delegate tasks; he abdicated responsibility for them because Joseph's competence was absolute. *"He left all that he had in Joseph's charge, and because of him he had no concern about anything but the food he ate"* (Genesis 39:6). Joseph created a "trust vacuum" that he filled with competence. He became indispensable not by seeking power, but by accepting responsibility. He proved that influence is not derived from position, but from the ability to solve problems that keep the leader awake at night.

The Immigrant Professional

Consider **Dr. Elena**.

In her home country of Venezuela, Elena was a pediatric neurosurgeon. She was published in international journals. She was respected. She saved lives daily. When political instability and violence forced her to flee to the United States, her credentials were not recognized. The "Transfer of Trust" didn't happen. The system saw a foreigner, not an expert.

She needed money to support her family while studying for the grueling USMLE steps—a process that would take years. She swallowed the bitter pill of pride and took a job as a phlebotomist in a busy, understaffed city hospital.

Imagine the psychological toll. She knows how to perform a craniotomy and how to map the brain, yet a tired, first-year resident is yelling at her for not labeling a blood vial correctly. The temptation to scream, *"Do you know who I am? I have performed surgeries you have only read about!"* is overwhelming. It is a daily assault on her ego. She is living in the gap between her capability and her reality—a state sociologists call **Status Dissonance**. She has high cultural capital (education) but low economic capital (job), creating a jarring internal conflict.

Elena chooses humility over entitlement. She adopts the mindset of a servant leader. She realizes that her "why"—healing people and alleviating suffering—hasn't changed, only the "how." The instrument has changed from a scalpel to a needle, but the heart remains the same.

She treats every patient drawing with the precision of a surgeon. She comforts terrified children with a bedside manner that the overworked doctors lack. She becomes the "informal leader" of the lab techs. She helps them organize their schedules. She teaches them Spanish medical terminology to help them communicate with the diverse patient population.

One day, a patient presents with subtle neurological symptoms that the rushing residents miss. There's a slight asymmetry in the smile, a barely noticeable tremor. Elena recognizes the signs of early-onset hydrocephalus. Quietly, respectfully, she flags a senior attending, suggesting a specific scan "just to be safe." Her intervention saves the patient's life. She didn't do it for credit; she did it for the patient.

Elena is learning the American medical system from the bottom up. She is observing insurance coding, patient intake flow, hospital bureaucracy, and nurse-doctor power dynamics—things she was blind to as a surgeon in her own country. She is building **Cultural Intelligence (CQ)**.

Three years later, Elena passes her boards and matches into a residency program. She is older than the other residents. But she is light-years ahead in maturity and perspective. When a crisis hits the ER, and the other residents panic, Elena is calm. She knows the system. She respects the nurses (and they respect her, because she was one of them). She possesses a **360-degree perspective** that her peers lack. Her season of obscurity in the lab made her a better leader than her season of prestige ever could.

The Prison Paradox

State Management in Solitary Confinement

The story of Joseph takes a dark, unjust turn. He does everything right (he maintains his sexual integrity with Potiphar's wife, fleeing temptation) and his reward is a false accusation of attempted rape and a prison sentence. This is the **Crucible of Injustice**.

For context, the prison Joseph entered was not a common jail. Genesis 39:20 calls it the "place where the king's prisoners were confined." This was the White House Prison, a high-security holding facility for political dissidents, fallen officials, and enemies of the state. This distinction is crucial: Joseph was not surrounded by common street thugs. He was incarcerated with the disgraced intelligentsia of Egypt—the cupbearer (head of security/protocol) and the baker (head of food safety).

If Potiphar's house was the undergraduate degree in economics and management, the king's prison was the PhD in political science and diplomacy. Here, Joseph would listen to court gossip, understand the whims of Pharaoh, and learn the intricate political web of Egypt. He was learning how the empire worked from the men who used to run it.

Network Theory and The Stockdale Paradox

In prison, Joseph had zero control over his environment. He could not leave. He could not appeal. He was faced with what Jim Collins calls the **Stockdale Paradox** (named after Admiral James Stockdale, a POW in Vietnam): *You must retain faith that you will prevail in the end, regardless of the difficulties, AND at the same time* *confront the most brutal facts of your current reality.*

Optimists died in the POW camps because they set arbitrary deadlines ("We will be out by Christmas") and died of a broken heart when those deadlines passed. Realists survived. Joseph didn't know *when* he would get out, but he decided *how* he would live while he was in.

Tony Robbins teaches that when you cannot control events, you must control your **Meaning**. Joseph faced a critical choice in how he framed his reality. The old meaning would have been a narrative of abandonment: *"God has abandoned me. I am a victim. My life is over."* However, Joseph chose a new meaning, one of agency and purpose: *"I am placed here to organize this chaos. I am the CEO of this dungeon."*

Genesis 39:22 says, *"So the keeper of the prison put Joseph in charge of all the prisoners who were in the prison."*

Joseph utilized **Network Theory**. He was leading from the middle of the node. Even though he had no title or authority, he still possessed influence. He controlled the flow of information and resources within the prison. He became the "informal organization" that made the formal organization function. He filled the structural holes in the prison's social network, connecting disparate groups and facilitating order.

He likely practiced what we now call **Cognitive Behavioral Therapy (CBT)** or **Neuro-Associative Conditioning**. He stopped associating pain with his surroundings and started associating pleasure with service. When the cupbearer and the baker were thrown into prison, Joseph noticed their distress. Genesis 40:7: *"So he asked Pharaoh's officers... 'Why are your faces downcast today?'"*

Think about that. Joseph is in the same hellhole they are, potentially facing a life sentence without parole, yet he has the emotional bandwidth to check on *their* mental state. This is **Strategic**

Empathy (a term used by Chris Voss). By diagnosing their emotional state, he unlocked their secrets (dreams), which eventually became his exit strategy. He served his way out of obscurity. This is the neuroscience of altruism: serving others triggers the release of oxytocin, which buffers the stress of one's own suffering.

Consider **David**.

David was a mid-level marketing manager in a major tech firm. He defined himself by his productivity, his salary, and his company perks. Then came the sector-wide layoffs. Weeks turned into months. The severance package ran out. The rejection emails piled up.

David entered the "Waiting Room." The loss of routine was destabilizing. He found himself doom-scrolling, his brain seeking dopamine hits from social media outrage because it wasn't getting them from work achievement. He felt the walls closing in. He began to question his worth, his talent, and his future.

David realized he was in a prison of his own making, a prison of passivity. He decided to apply the **"Joseph Prison Protocol."**

First, he moved to **Structure the Chaos**. He treated his job hunt like a job, establishing a rigid schedule with a 9 AM start and 5 PM finish. He showered, dressed up, and went to the library to work. He refused to let the entropy of unemployment consume his discipline. He created a routine to replace the one he lost.

Second, he began to serve the fellow prisoners. David realized many of his colleagues were also laid off and struggling with depression and loss of direction. He started a weekly Zoom mastermind called "The Pivot." He didn't charge for it. He just facilitated. He helped them fix their resumes. He brought in guest speakers. He listened to their venting. He connected people. He became a conduit of resources for others, even though he had no "resources" of his own. He realized that even when his bank account was empty, his *network and intellectual capital remained* valuable assets he could deploy.

In the process of serving others, David discovered a latent talent. He wasn't just a marketing manager; he was a gifted coach and community builder. He began writing about his journey on LinkedIn—not from a place of desperation ("Please hire me"), but from a place of shared struggle and value ("Here is how we are surviving").

David never went back to a traditional marketing job. One of the members of his mastermind group got hired as a director at a major firm and brought David in as a head of people and culture. David's time in the "prison" of unemployment gave him the empathy and the organizational skills to lead the human side of a business—skills he never would have developed in the comfort of his old role. He learned that his value was not in his job title, but in his ability to serve and connect.

The Convergence of Preparedness and Opportunity

Joseph was seventeen when he went in. He was thirty when he came out. Thirteen years of the Hidden Curriculum. Thirteen years of silence. Two of those years occurred *after* he interpreted the cupbearer's dream. The text says the cupbearer "forgot him." Those two years of silence were likely the hardest test of all, the test of being forgotten by man but remembered by God.

When Pharaoh had a disturbing dream that no one could interpret, Joseph was summoned from the dungeon. Note the text: *"They quickly brought him out of the pit. And when he had shaved himself and changed his clothes, he came in before Pharaoh."* (Genesis 41:14).

He was ready. He *adapted.* He shaved, removing his Hebrew beard, which was an abomination to Egyptians. He put on clean clothes. He respected the protocol of the court he was about to address. If Joseph had been pulled out of the pit at age eighteen, he would have failed. He might have interpreted the dream (a spiritual gift), but he would not have had the administrative capacity, the emotional maturity, or the strategic foresight to manage the solution. The "Hidden Curriculum" had prepared him for this exact moment. He had learned the language of the court, the economics of the estate, and the politics of the prison.

Strategy and Supply Chain Resilience

The interpretation of the dream (seven years of plenty, seven years of famine) was only 10% of the solution. Any mystic could have given a prediction. The other 90% was logistics. Joseph instantly pivoted from Prophet to Technocrat. He didn't just identify the problem; he architected the solution.

He proposed a specific, actionable policy: *"Let Pharaoh proceed to appoint overseers over the land and take one-fifth of the produce of the land of Egypt during the seven plenteous years."* (Genesis 41:34).

Joseph invented **Counter-Cyclical Fiscal Policy** and **Antifragility** (a concept by Nassim Taleb, systems that benefit from disorder). His strategy relied on two robust pillars. First, he implemented a 20% tax during the years of surplus. This rate was carefully calculated, high enough to build massive reserves but low enough to encourage continued production without stifling the farmers. It was a sustainable extraction rate that prioritized delayed gratification on a national scale. Second, he utilized regional warehousing by storing the grain *in* the cities where it was harvested (Gen 41:48). This decentralized supply chain management was a masterstroke. By refusing to haul everything to a central capital, he avoided logistical bottlenecks, reduced transport costs, and minimized the risk of spoilage or pest infestation. This distributed system ensured local food security and resilience against regional failures. Unlike modern "Just-in-Time" supply chains that are brittle and break under stress, Joseph built a "Just-in-Case" system designed for deep resilience.

Maxwell's The Law of the Lid had been lifted. Joseph's leadership ability had been forged in the fire, so his effectiveness could now scale to the level of a nation. He saved the known world from starvation because he had learned to manage a household and a prison.

God Meant It For Good

When Joseph finally reveals himself to his brothers years later, he says the famous words: *"As for you, you meant evil against me, but God meant it for good."* (Genesis 50:20).

This is the ultimate **Cognitive Reframing**. Neuroscience tells us that the brain seeks coherence. We need our life story to make sense. Psychologists like Dan McAdams distinguish between "contamination sequences" (where good things go bad) and "redemption sequences" (where bad things are redeemed). Leaders who possess **Narrative Identity**, the ability to construct a redemptive story out of their trauma, are more resilient and effective.

Joseph's brain had physically changed. The neural pathways of resentment and victimhood had been pruned away through disuse. The pathways of strategic foresight, empathy, trust in Providence, and resilience had been myelinated—supercharged for speed and efficiency. He was no longer the fragile boy in the coat; he was the antifragile ruler of Egypt. He had the power to execute his brothers, but he chose to feed them. This is the final exam of the curriculum: **Power under Control**.

My Thoughts

You may be in the pit. You may be in Potiphar's house. You may be in prison. You are not lost. You are in school.

The Hidden Curriculum is mandatory, but passing the final exam is optional. You can grow bitter, or you can grow better. You can emerge from this season with a chip on your shoulder, or you can emerge with a mantle of authority.

Who can you serve today, right where you are? Stop looking at the org chart. Look at the human being next to you. If you are in the mailroom, be the best mailroom clerk in history. If you are unemployed, serve your family with excellence. Build trust in the small things.

Check your state. Are you slouching in defeat? Stand up. Change your physiology. Change your focus from what you have lost to what you are learning. What skill are you mastering in the dark? Are you building the muscle of faith that will sustain you in the light? Decide to be the master of your meaning.

Lead yourself. If you cannot lead yourself in the boredom of obscurity, you cannot lead a team in the pressure of the spotlight. Character is the only foundation that can support the weight of success. Use this time to deepen your foundation.

Do not despise the day of small beginnings. Do not rush the process. Let the Hidden Curriculum do its work. Let it scour the pride from your heart. Let it build the muscle of your character. Because the palace is coming. The famine is coming. And the world doesn't need more charismatic celebrities with hollow characters. It needs **Josephs**. It needs leaders who have been vetted by the dark, seasoned by the struggle, and prepared to save many people alive.

Stay in the class. Pass the test.

The "Hard Season" Audit

Take ten minutes to reflect on the following prompts. Identify which season you are currently navigating: the Pit (marked by trauma and shock), Potiphar's House (defined by grinding and serving), or Prison (characterized by unjust waiting). Consider the **Skill Gap** by identifying one specific "hard skill," such as financial literacy, coding, writing, or logistics, that you can learn during this downtime, which you might not have time for otherwise. Next, examine the **Character Gap** by pinpointing one "soft skill," like patience, humility, listening, or empathy, that God seems to be pressing on, and recognize where your ego is being challenged. Finally, plan a **Service Pivot** by looking for those who are suffering around you. Determine how you can help them today, even with your limited resources, and who you can lift up while you are waiting to be lifted.

If you are navigating a high-stakes transition and want to apply this framework to your own situation with clarity and discipline, scan the QR code below for a Transition Readiness Chat.

CHAPTER 4

Integrity Under Autonomy: Leading Ethically When No One Is Watching

"Character is what you do when no one is watching."

— John Wooden

The Audience of One

Leadership is influence, nothing more, nothing less. But the *sustainability* of that influence is entirely dependent on the structural integrity of the leader's soul. We live in an era obsessed with the optics of leadership, the stage presence, the viral soundbite, the quarterly growth chart, and the carefully curated public persona. We have created a culture of "Avatar Leadership," where the digital projection of a leader often bears little resemblance to the human reality behind the screen. We mistake the platform for the person, assuming that visibility equals viability. We think of leadership as what happens when we stand in front of a crowd, with the lights on and the stakes public. But the true test of a leader—the crucible where the "gold" of character is refined—happens in the dark, in the quiet spaces where no applause can reach.

We call this **Integrity in Isolation**.

Imagine an iceberg floating in the North Atlantic. We all know the analogy where only ten percent is visible above the water, representing your public skills, charisma, and results. This is the part that gets the promotions, the accolades, and the book deals. However, the remaining ninety percent is hidden beneath the surface, comprised of your character, values, discipline, secret habits, and the internal monologue that governs your decisions when you are alone. But here is the physics of the iceberg that most leaders miss: *The submerged ninety percent determines the stability of the visible 10%.* The center of gravity is deep underwater. It is the density of the hidden ice that keeps the peak upright against the wind and waves. If the ice beneath the water fractures, melts, or shifts due to the warming waters of compromise, the center of gravity changes catastrophically. The tip doesn't just sink; it flips over violently.

In our current cultural moment, we are witnessing a pandemic of "flipped icebergs." We see CEOs, pastors, politicians, and influencers who possess immense public talent but lack private substance. They stood tall for a season, but their foundations were hollowed out by secret compromises—small ethical erosions that went unnoticed until the structural failure was total. They didn't fail because they lost their skill; they failed because they lost their structural density. They collapsed not because of external pressure, but because of internal hollowness. They lacked the private infrastructure to support the crushing weight of their public elevation.

This chapter explores the life of Joseph, a young man who mastered the art of leading himself when no one was watching. We will dissect the anatomy of his integrity in Genesis 39 as a masterclass in leadership ethics, ancient sociology, and emotional maturity. We will see that private character is the actual engine that powers public elevation.

If you cannot lead yourself in the empty room, you are not ready to lead others in the boardroom.

The Joseph Paradox: Authority Without Title

To understand Integrity in Isolation, we must look at the high-stakes context of Joseph's test. The narrative in Genesis 39 places Joseph in a situation of utter dislocation. He is stripped of his coat, which symbolized his father's favor; he is stripped of his family, which provided his identity; and he is stripped of his freedom, which provided his agency. He transitioned from the "Prince of Canaan" to a piece of property in a foreign market. He is sold into slavery in Egypt, the superpower of the ancient world. He is purchased by Potiphar, the captain of the guard—a man of immense political and military weight who likely served as the chief of Pharaoh's executioners and security forces.

The psychological shock of this transition cannot be overstated. Most people in Joseph's position would have succumbed to the victim mentality, paralyzed by trauma and bitterness. It is the default human response to injustice to say, "The system is broken, so why should I play by the rules?" Yet, Joseph refused to let his circumstances define his character. He understood a principle that Viktor Frankl would articulate thousands of years later: everything can be taken from a man but one thing—the last of the human freedoms—to choose one's attitude in any given set of circumstances.

John C. Maxwell often refers to the **Law of the Lid**, stating that leadership ability determines a person's level of effectiveness. But Joseph proves a critical corollary to this law: **The Law of Solid Ground**. Trust is the foundation of leadership, and Joseph built this foundation before he ever had a platform. He has no civil rights, no salary, and no title other than "slave." He is a line item in a ledger. Yet, the text tells us something profound regarding his trajectory:

"The Lord was with Joseph, and he was a successful man... So Joseph found favor in his sight and attended him, and he made him overseer of his house and put him in charge of all that he had." (Genesis 39:2, 4)

Joseph didn't wait for a promotion to start acting with excellence. He didn't say, "Well, once they stop treating me like a piece of property, then I'll show them my management skills." He led with excellence within the confines of his restriction. He understood that while he could not control his circumstances, he had absolute sovereignty over his response. He transformed his slavery into a stewardship, proving that true leadership is not a function of position but of disposition. He realized that excellence is a language that transcends culture and status; even in Egypt, quality work could not be ignored.

The Leadership Vacuum & The ABCD Model

Potiphar was a powerful man, likely consumed with state affairs, military campaigns, and court intrigue. Like many high-level executives today, he had a "leadership vacuum" in his domestic affairs. He was too busy running the empire's security to manage the grain inventories, the livestock, or the staff disputes of his own estate. He needed someone he could trust explicitly—a proxy who could act with his authority and think with his mind. Joseph filled that vacuum by embodying what Ken Blanchard calls the **ABCD Model of Trust**, a framework that turns competence into credibility.

First, Joseph proved he was **Able**. He was not just good; he was exceptional. Under his watch, the house ran efficiently, resources were optimized, waste was reduced, and order was established. He demonstrated professional mastery that made him indispensable. He likely learned the Egyptian language, mastered the complex accounting systems of the Nile economy, and managed a large staff of other servants. He turned chaos into systems. When Potiphar asked for a report, Joseph had the numbers. When a crisis arose in the fields, Joseph had a solution before Potiphar even knew there was a problem.

Second, he was **Believable**. He acted with transparency and integrity. His "Yes" was "Yes," and he refused to hide mistakes or manipulate the books for personal gain. In a culture where skimming off the top was likely common among servants—a "tax" for their service—Joseph's books were impeccable. He operated in the light, even when no one was looking. He understood that trust is gained in drops and lost in buckets, so he guarded his credibility fiercely.

Third, he was **Connected**. He demonstrated empathy and cared about the success of the household. He wasn't a mercenary; he treated Potiphar's assets as if they were his own inheritance. He aligned his personal success with the success of his master, creating a symbiotic relationship rather than an adversarial one. He didn't just serve Potiphar; he served Potiphar's interests. He likely knew the names of the other servants, mediated their disputes, and built a culture of morale within the estate.

Finally, he was **Dependable**. He was consistent. His behavior didn't fluctuate based on whether Potiphar was in the room or away at the palace. This consistency is the bedrock of trust. Potiphar eventually realized that he didn't need to audit Joseph; he simply needed to empower him. This level of trust creates a dangerous, seductive power: *Autonomy.*

Autonomy is the playground of integrity. *When you are micromanaged, your behavior is shaped by compliance—you do it because you are being watched. When you are autonomous, your behavior is shaped by character—you do it because of who you are.* Joseph was in a foreign land, separated from his father, Jacob, from the covenant community, and from the cultural accountability of his upbringing. He was anonymous. He could have reinvented his morality to match his new geography, adopting the ethics of Egypt to survive. Instead, he imported the ethics of heaven to thrive.

The Geography of Temptation

To truly grasp the magnitude of Joseph's temptation, we must look at the archaeology of an Egyptian noble's estate during the Middle Kingdom period (roughly 2000–1700 B.C.). We need to visualize the "stage" to understand the pressure. This was not a small apartment; it was a sprawling, self-contained city block designed to project power and wealth.

Excavations at sites like Kahun reveal that wealthy Egyptian villas were vast, complex compounds, often exceeding ten thousand square feet. They were designed with distinct, segregated zones to manage the social hierarchy of the time. There was a **Public Reception Area**, a bustling zone where business was conducted, scribes worked, and guests were entertained. This area would have been filled with noise, movement, and witnesses. It was the zone of accountability. The walls were painted with bright murals, and the floors were busy with the traffic of commerce.

Distinct from this were the **Inner Private Quarters**, containing the harem and family living spaces. These areas were architecturally designed for privacy and seclusion, often separated from the rest of the house by a thick mud-brick wall and a single, guarded door. Access to this zone was strictly controlled; it was a "sanctum sanctorum" of domestic life, shaded from the sun, quiet, and scented with incense.

Joseph's title, often translated as "Overseer," corresponds to the Egyptian title *Mer-Per* (Overseer of the House). The *Mer-Per* was not a field hand; he was the Chief of Staff. Archaeological evidence, such as the Brooklyn Papyrus, confirms that Asiatic servants like Joseph rose to positions of high domestic trust in this era, often managing complex supply chains of linen, grain, and livestock.

Crucially, the *Mer-Per* was one of the few males (perhaps the *only* male besides Potiphar) allowed access to the inner magazines located deep within the private quarters to inventory grain, linen, and precious oils.

This provides the "physical stage" for the drama. The "empty house" described in Genesis wasn't an accident; it was a feature of the architecture. The master was out, the other servants were likely in the outer workshops or fields, and Joseph's duties required him to be in the private zone—the domain of the mistress. This was not a temptation of happenstance; it was a temptation of **structural privilege**. Joseph's integrity was tested exactly where his competence had placed him. The very keys that proved his success opened the door to his destruction.

The Invitation to Compromise

Enter Potiphar's wife. The text describes a relentless pursuit. She cast her eyes on Joseph and said, "Lie with me."

This wasn't a one-time offer; it was a siege. "Day after day," she spoke to him. It was a war of attrition. We must strip away the caricature of this story. This wasn't just about sexual temptation, though that was certainly present. This was a temptation of **power** and **expediency**.

First, it was a **Power Play**. Sleeping with the master's wife would have solidified Joseph's status in the house. It was a "strategic merger" for security. In the ancient world, sexual access often equated to political leverage. By aligning himself with the mistress of the house, Joseph could have secured his position against any other rivals in the household. It was a shortcut to unshakeable job security. It was an insurance policy against Potiphar's potential displeasure.

Second, she offered the **Safety of Secrecy**. She essentially told him, "No one will know." The house was empty. The thick walls of the Egyptian villa ensured silence. It was the perfect crime. The argument was likely sophisticated: "Potiphar is always away. He neglects me. You run this house anyway; you deserve the privileges of the master. Who are you hurting? We both have needs." It was a temptation to rationalize entitlement. It was the subtle whisper that rules are for the common people, but exceptions are for the elite.

Joseph's refusal is one of the greatest leadership statements in history. He does not equivocate. He does not negotiate. He does not flirt with the boundary.

"Behold, because of me, my master has no concern about anything in the house... he is not greater in this house than I am, nor has he kept back anything from me except you, because you are his wife. How then could I do this great evil and sin against God?" (Genesis 39:8-9)

Notice his logic. He appeals to three pillars of ethical leadership. He begins with **Stewardship**, acknowledging that "My master trusts me." He recognizes that his power is delegated, not owned. He refuses to use the master's resources (including his wife) for his own gratification. He moves to **Boundaries**, reminding her, "You are his wife." He respects the structural boundaries of the relationship, defining reality in a moment when she tried to blur the lines. Finally, he anchors his decision in **Theology**, calling it a "Sin against God." He elevates the crime from a social misdemeanor or a breach of contract to a spiritual treason. He realized that the most important person in the room was the One who is invisible.

The Empty House

The "Empty House" of Potiphar has just changed forms. The dynamics of autonomy, secrecy, and opportunity remain the same.

Let's look at three modern mirrors of this narrative through the lens of modern management and strategy, expanding on the psychological toll of these temptations.

The Remote Employee in the Digital Wilderness

Consider **Jane**, a talented software developer working 100% remotely.

Her boss is in a different time zone, and as long as she commits her code by Friday, no one asks questions. She is operating in a high-trust, low-oversight environment. The "walls" of her house are the Slack channels and Zoom rooms that only show what she wants them to show. She is the master of her digital domain.

The temptation she faces is the **"Quiet Quit"** or "Cyber-Loafing." It is the slow drift into doing the bare minimum, perhaps using a mouse jiggler to keep her status "Green" while she watches Netflix. It is the belief that "if the output is met, the input doesn't matter." This is not just laziness; it is a crisis of professional identity. It is the subtle corrosion of the work ethic that claims, "I am only worth what you can catch me doing." It transforms work from a vocation into a transaction, and eventually, into a con. It is the loss of professional dignity, replaced by the anxious cleverness of getting away with it.

Management often falls into a trap here, responding with surveillance software such as keyloggers or screen captures, which undermines trust and compliance. This creates a cat-and-mouse game that kills culture. But Jane faces her own "Joseph Trap," feeling entitled to slack off because she is efficient and believes the wealthy company won't miss her discretionary effort. She justifies the theft of time by pointing to the company's profits, convincing herself that she is merely balancing the scales.

The strategic pivot requires **Outcome-Based Integrity**. This distinguishes between *Transactional Work* (doing the minimum for the check) and *Covenantal Work* (honoring the agreement with excellence). If Jane applies the Joseph principle, she realizes that "Ethical Fading" starts small. A long lunch becomes a skipped afternoon, which eventually becomes a missed deadline. When she chooses to give 100% in the dark—to refactor the code no one will see—she is building capacity. As Ken Blanchard notes, "Integrity is what you do when no one is watching; legacy is what happens because you did." She must realize that even when unseen, she is in training. Every line of code written with excellence is a deposit into her own future competency. She is not working for the company; she is working for her own potential.

Consider **Evander.**

Pastor Evander leads a mid-sized church. He is ambitious and wants to reach his city, but he feels small when comparing himself to the "megachurch" leaders on Instagram with their viral clips and book deals. He feels the existential dread of irrelevance in a marketplace of attention. He worries that if he doesn't grow, he is failing God.

He faces the temptation of the marketing agency that promises to "explode his growth" using algorithms, bot farms, and sensationalized clips. They suggest he soften his theological stance to lower barriers to entry, framing it as "modernization" rather than compromise. They offer to buy him a platform rather than help him build a people. This is the temptation of **Expediency over Effectiveness**. It is Potiphar's wife offering a shortcut to growth that bypasses the covenant of truth, promising the reward of influence without the requisite labor of discipleship. It promises the harvest without the plowing.

Evander is in the "Empty House" of leadership, where his board trusts him and likely won't scrutinize the metrics too closely. He must choose between ego leadership, which demands numbers to validate self-worth, and servant leadership, which refuses to sacrifice the long-term health of the flock for the short-term high of the crowd. Declining the hype machine means accepting slower growth and the unglamorous work of discipleship. It feels like obscurity, but the integrity of the pulpit is the only thing that sustains the power of the Gospel. A platform built on hype has no foundation for the storms of crisis; it is a house of cards waiting for a stiff wind. Evander must realize that God counts weight, not just numbers. When the crisis comes, the "bot-farmed" followers will vaporize, but the disciples built in integrity will stand.

Consider **Helene.**

Helene is a twenty-eight-year-old executive, brilliant and committed to her faith. She meets Will, who is successful, kind, and wealthy, but does not share her values regarding faith or physical boundaries.

The pressure she faces is **Compromise through Fear**. She hears the whisper, "Refuse me, and life will get hard for you," or the internal fear, "Refuse this, and you will be alone forever." Helene is in the empty room with just her desires and the fear of scarcity. The temptation is to compartmentalize her faith, to convince herself that she can change him later, or that her standards are archaic. She is tempted to trade her birthright for a bowl of stew, prioritizing immediate connection over eternal alignment. She justifies it by saying, "He is a good man," ignoring the fundamental misalignment of their souls.

From a strategic standpoint, this is a "Bad Merger." In business, a merger with a partner whose core values are incompatible always leads to mission drift and eventual dissolution. Will offers short-term capital in the form of companionship, but threatens the long-term mission statement of her life. The initial synergy will eventually give way to a culture clash that destroys the entity.

Joseph knew that losing his coat was better than losing his conscience, so he fled. For Helene, "fleeing" is an act of strategic avoidance. It is the refusal to trade long-term peace for short-term intimacy. It requires the emotional maturity to do the right thing even when she feels like doing the wrong thing, understanding that being "unequally yoked" is a recipe for structural collapse. It is the bravery to choose holy loneliness over compromised company, trusting that God is better at writing her love story than she is at forcing it.

Why does this matter?

Why shouldn't we just take the shortcut if the result is "good"? Why not use the bots to grow the church? Why not quit if the job gets done? To answer this, we must look at the internal mechanics of character.

The Muscle Memory of Righteousness

Joseph didn't decide to have integrity the moment Potiphar's wife grabbed him. That would have been too late. The adrenaline of the moment would have overwhelmed an unformed will. He decided it years before, in the small, unrecorded moments of his life. Neuroscience tells us that every time we resist an impulse, we strengthen the prefrontal cortex—the executive center of the brain responsible for long-term planning and impulse control. Conversely, every time we yield to immediate gratification, we strengthen the limbic system, the primitive "reward" center.

We are constantly carving neural pathways. Imagine a sled going down a snowy hill; the first time is hard, but the second time, the sled naturally follows the groove of the first run. By the tenth time, it is almost impossible to steer out of the groove. Joseph had "reps" in the gym of integrity. He had said "no" to small entitlements and small compromises thousands of times before. When the heavy weight of this temptation dropped on him, his spiritual muscles reacted. This is the concept of **Neuroplasticity of Virtue**. You cannot forge character in a crisis; you can only reveal it. Crisis does not make the leader; it exposes the leader. If you cheat in the practice round, you will cheat in the tournament.

The Dungeon as a Leadership Incubator

Here is the counterintuitive strategy of the Kingdom: *The descent into the dungeon is often the prerequisite for the ascent to the throne.*

Joseph did the right thing and got the wrong result. He was falsely accused and thrown into prison. This is the moment most leaders quit, feeling punished for following the rules. They become bitter, cynical, and victimized. They ask, "If God is good, why am I here?" But Genesis 39:21 reminds us, *"But the Lord was with Joseph."* In prison, Joseph became the manager of the prison, mastering the art of **Leading Without a Title**.

Archaeologically, this was not a common pit, but the *Beit Sohar*—the Round House, a fortress prison reserved for the king's prisoners. This creates a fascinating implication: Joseph wasn't mixing with common thieves. He was likely incarcerated with disgraced court officials, political dissidents, spies, and high-ranking state enemies. This was an elite holding tank for the intelligentsia of Egypt who had fallen out of favor.

This was his "graduate school." In this elite confinement, he learned court protocol and how to speak to nobility. He gained political intelligence by understanding the factions and power dynamics of Egypt. He practiced crisis management by handling the egos of fallen leaders. He learned to interpret not just dreams, but people. These were the exact skills he would need when he eventually stood before Pharaoh to save the world from famine. God used the dungeon to refine the raw material of Joseph's talent into the steel of statesmanship.

History reflects this pattern. Nelson Mandela spent twenty-seven years in prison, yet he led the anti-apartheid movement *from his cell*. Steve Jobs was fired from Apple, and his "wilderness years" at

NeXT and Pixar were where he learned the patience and maturity that eventually saved Apple. The dungeon is not a graveyard; it is a classroom. It is where God strips away the reliance on talent and builds a reliance on character.

If Joseph had slept with Potiphar's wife, he might have stayed a *comfortable slave* in a rich man's house. He would have had a comfortable bed and good food, but he never would have developed the capacity to rule a nation. His "No" in the bedroom was the key to his "Yes" in the palace. He proved he could handle power without being corrupted by it.

Building Your Dungeon Walls

How do we build this kind of integrity today? We need more than good intentions; we need a management strategy for our souls. We need to operationalize integrity through the "Three P's" of Private Purity.

Pre-Decision (Strategic Planning): You must decide before the moment comes. This is what psychologists call "implementation intentions" or an "if-then" plan for your willpower. Joseph had a theological framework *before* the woman approached him. He didn't have to debate the pros and cons in the heat of passion; the decision had already been made. This conserves "willpower energy" for execution rather than deliberation.

- **For the remote worker:** "I will work from 9:00 to 5:00 and will not bill for hours I did not work. If I finish early, I will study or ask for more work, not slack off."
- **For the leader:** "I will never be alone in a room with a member of the opposite sex who is not my spouse," or "I will not sign a check that I haven't reviewed."
- **For the student:** "I will accept a lower grade rather than cheat. My integrity is worth more than my GPA."

By pre-deciding, you remove decision fatigue from the moment of temptation. You are simply executing a pre-approved protocol.

Protective Barriers (Risk Management): Joseph refused to even "be with her" (Gen 39:10). He managed his proximity. He recognized that willpower is a finite resource, so he relied on structural barriers. He didn't trust his own strength; he trusted his systems.

- **Digitally:** Install blockers like Freedom or Opal on your devices. Share your browsing history with an accountability partner. Turn off notifications that trigger distraction.
- **Relationally:** Change your route to the coffee machine. Ensure the door is left open during meetings. Avoid late-night text conversations with colleagues.
- **Financially:** Create dual-signature requirements for expenses. Separate personal and business accounts rigidly.

If you know you are weak in an area, build a wall, not a door. Don't rely on your brakes; rely on the guardrails.

Perspective of the Eternal (Vision Casting): Joseph viewed his actions through the lens of "Sin against God." He reframed the temptation. It wasn't just a horizontal breach of contract with Potiphar; it was a vertical breach of covenant with Yahweh.

Practice the presence of God in your daily work. This is the ancient concept of *Coram Deo*—living before the face of God. Before you open your laptop or enter a meeting, pray a simple prayer: *"Lord, you are in this room. Let my work be an act of worship to You."* Turn your workspace into a sanctuary. When you realize the Audience of One is watching, the applause of the crowd loses its allure, and the secrecy of the empty room loses its power. You are no longer performing for an audience that can be fooled; you are serving a Master who knows the heart.

My Reflection

We live in a world desperate for leaders who are the same in the dark as they are in the light. We are tired of the scandals, the hypocrisy, and the "flipped icebergs." We are cynical because we have been disappointed too many times by charisma without character. We are starving for the Josephs—men and women who possess a gravitas that cannot be purchased, only forged.

To the remote worker fighting the drift of laziness in a silent apartment: Your integrity is building a work ethic that will one day carry heavy responsibilities. You are building the muscle of self-governance. Keep typing. God sees you.

To the pastor refusing the sugar rush of hype and the allure of the viral clip: Your integrity is building a church that will stand when the cultural winds shift, and the trends fade. You are building on rock, not sand. Keep preaching the Word. God hears you.

To the young professional standing firm in your values against the pressure to compromise for connection: Your integrity is protecting your future legacy. You are preserving your soul for the right partner and the right mission. Keep standing. God is with you.

The promise is this: Private character is the engine of public elevation. It may not happen on your timeline. You may have to spend time in the dungeon of obscurity. You may feel forgotten. But God is a master architect. He never builds the superstructure higher than the foundation can support. He is digging deep in you now so He can build high through you later.

Build deep. Walk straight. Live true.

The world is watching, even when you think no one is there. But more importantly, so is He.

Calls to Action

For the Head (Think): Read Genesis 39 this week and conduct an audit of your "Empty Rooms." Identify where you have total autonomy and ask yourself if your standards there are higher or lower than your public standards. Furthermore, conduct a "Trust Audit" using the ABCD model by asking a trusted colleague where you are strong and where you are weak.

For the Heart (Feel): Do you feel the resentment of the "Dungeon," feeling punished for doing good? Do you feel like you've been forgotten by God? Bring that emotion to Him. Ask Him to turn your bitterness into endurance. Remember that the dungeon is a classroom, not a graveyard.

For the Hands (Do): Implement an "Open Door" Policy, either literally or digitally. Invite accountability into your isolated spaces this week by sharing your screen, opening your calendar, or confessing a small struggle to a friend before it becomes a large failure. Finally, create a "Code of Conduct." Write a personal manifesto for your work and life, sign it, date it, and keep it visible.

If you are navigating a high-stakes transition and want to apply this framework to your own situation with clarity and discipline, scan the QR code below for a Transition Readiness Chat.

CHAPTER 5

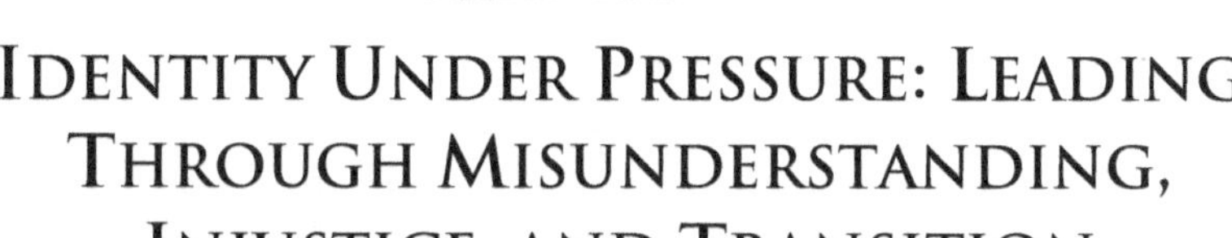

Identity Under Pressure: Leading Through Misunderstanding, Injustice, and Transition

"To be in a liminal state is to be on a threshold where the old world is gone, but the new world is not yet here."

— William Bridges

The Liminal Space of Leadership

The heavy wooden door slams shut, and the iron bolt slides home with a finality that vibrates in your chest. The sound is not just mechanical; it is existential. It marks the precise boundary between the life you built and the void you now inhabit. The air is stale, heavy with the scent of damp earth, unwashed bodies, and the acrid tang of despair. The darkness is almost physical, pressing against your eyes like a blindfold. Just hours ago, you were the trusted steward of Potiphar's house, managing vast wealth, making high-stakes decisions, and walking in impeccable integrity. Now, you are merely number forty-two in the king's dungeon.

You did the right thing. You ran from sin. You held the standard high when compromise would have been easier. You refused to leverage your position for personal pleasure. And your reward was not a promotion, a bonus, or a public accolade; it was a pit.

This is the **Prison of Misunderstanding.**

In narrative theory and depth psychology, this location is known as a *liminal space*, derived from the Latin *limen*, meaning "threshold." It is the disorienting "nowhere" between an old identity that is gone and a new one that has not yet arrived. It is the Saturday between Good Friday and Easter Sunday. It is the silence between the prayer and the answer.

It is perhaps the most psychologically grueling location in the landscape of leadership because it lacks clear coordinates. It is that season where your motives are maligned, your hard work is ignored, and your reputation is stained by a narrative you did not write and cannot control. It is the dissonance of knowing *who* you are while the world tells you *what* you are, and the two do not match.

We all know the macro-narrative of Joseph, the coat of many colors, the dreamer, the eventual Prime Minister of Egypt who saves the known world from famine. But we often rush past the middle chapters. We skip from the pit to the palace because the prison is uncomfortable. We prefer the coronation to the confinement. We want the strategy for the throne room without the stamina for the dungeon. We want the authority without the anonymity. We want the influence without the injustice.

However, if we adopt the lens of effective leadership, peak performance psychology, and historical context, we realize that the prison was not a detour. It was the incubator. It was the crucible where the dross of youthful arrogance was burned away to reveal the gold of seasoned character. The prison is where the "Dreamer" became the "Administrator." It is where the pampered son became the suffering servant. It is where the theory of faith became the theology of resilience.

In this chapter, we are going deep into the dungeon of Genesis 39 and 40. We will excavate the archaeological reality of an Egyptian prison, deconstruct the neuroscience of rejection and betrayal, apply the "Law of Process," and examine three modern leaders who are currently sitting in that same cell. If you feel forgotten, if you feel misrepresented, or if you feel like you've been buried, take heart. You haven't been buried. You've been planted.

The Anatomy of Injustice

To understand the weight of Joseph's trial, we must strip away the sanitized Sunday School images of a jail cell with bars and a cot. We must understand the brutal reality of the setting. Genesis 39:20 uses a specific, rare Hebrew phrase, *Bayt HaSohar*, often translated as "prison," but literally meaning "The Round House" or "The Fortress."

Egyptian prisons of the Middle Kingdom were not merely holding cells; they were often converted granaries or underground silos—circular, deep, and structurally designed to contain grain, not humans. Imagine a cylinder dug into the earth, perhaps fifteen to twenty feet deep, with a single opening at the top for light and air. They were designed to strip a man of his orientation through sensory deprivation. Ventilation was poor, and light was scarce. The temperature fluctuated wildly between the scorching heat of the day and the biting cold of the desert night. The sensory environment was designed to break the will, offering no windows to the horizon, only a glimpse of the sky far above—a taunting reminder of the freedom lost.

Furthermore, the social hierarchy of this prison was distinct. As previously discussed, this was the *place of the king's prisoners*, a high-security facility reserved for political dissidents, failed assassins, and high-ranking officials who had fallen out of favor. Joseph was thrown into a political holding tank with the state's most dangerous inconveniences, meaning his cellmates were likely educated, dangerous, and desperate.

This matters immensely because it means the stakes were life and death. In this darkness, the silence is loud, and the threat of execution hangs heavy in the stagnant air. Every time the grate at the top opened, Joseph didn't know if he was receiving bread or a death sentence. He was isolated from his family, his culture, and his God's apparent favor, trapped in a silo of silence.

Identity Dissonance and the Scapegoat

Genesis 39:19-20 tells us: *"So it was, when his master heard the words which his wife spoke to him... his anger was aroused. Then Joseph's master took him and put him into the prison."*

Psychologically, the transition from "trusted steward" to "accused rapist" causes a fracture in the human psyche known as **Identity Dissonance**. We all carry an internal script of who we are. For Joseph, that script read: *I am a man of God, a man of honor, a faithful servant.* When his external reality (chained prisoner) violently contradicted his internal reality (man of integrity), his brain would have triggered a massive threat response.

Neuroscientists have found that social rejection, reputation loss, and public shaming activate the anterior cingulate cortex—the exact same region that registers a burn or a broken bone. The brain does not distinguish between "my leg is broken" and "my reputation is destroyed," registering both as immediate survival threats. The pain of betrayal is not metaphorical; it is physiological. This triggers an "Amygdala Hijack," where the emotional center of the brain overwhelms the prefrontal cortex, flooding the system with cortisol and making strategic thinking nearly impossible. The natural response is to fight with rage against the accuser or freeze into depression and catatonia.

Joseph is suffering from the acute trauma of *misunderstanding*. The "Just World Hypothesis"—the psychological bias that assumes good things happen to good people and bad things happen to bad people—has been shattered. He is confronting the terrifying reality that righteousness does not guarantee safety. This is the moment where many leaders break, succumbing to cynicism and believing that *if the system is rigged, integrity is a fool's game.*

The Corporate Scapegoat

Let's bring this into the boardroom to see how this ancient trauma manifests today. Meet Michael.

Michael is a senior project manager at a high-velocity tech firm. For eighteen months, he has poured his lifeblood into "Project Aether." He worked late nights, optimized the budget to save the company 15%, mentored junior developers, and flagged a critical compliance risk early in the process. His boss, a charismatic but disorganized VP, waved off the risk, telling Michael to "stop being a blocker" and "just get it shipped."

When the compliance audit fails and the stock price dips, the VP triggers what organizational sociologists call the **Scapegoat Mechanism**. Developed by philosopher René Girard, this theory posits that groups, when threatened with internal disintegration or external pressure, often unify by expelling a single victim. To maintain social cohesion and protect the hierarchy, the VP pivots.

In the boardroom, the VP looks at the CEO and says, "It's unfortunate. I gave Michael autonomy, but it seems the project leadership lost focus on regulatory standards. We need fresh eyes." Michael sits there, stunned. The air leaves the room. He tries to speak, to point to the emails where he flagged the risk, but the narrative has already solidified. He is the problem. The group sighs in relief; they have found the cancer, and now they can cut it out. They avoid eye contact with him, implicitly agreeing to the lie to save their own skins.

The aftermath is swift and silent. Michael is quietly called into HR. He isn't fired, that would require cause and paperwork, but he is erased. He is removed from the project he built and reassigned to "Special Projects"—corporate code for a dead-end desk with no budget, no team, and no influence. He returns to his desk to find his access to key files revoked and his calendar, once full of strategy sessions, suddenly empty. His colleagues, who know the truth but fear for their own mortgages and stock options, say nothing. They avert their eyes in the hallway.

The silence of the team is more painful than the betrayal of the boss. Michael is in the Round House. He looks around his windowless office and thinks, *I did everything right. Why is this happening?* The silence of his phone is deafening. He questions his competence, his judgment, and his future, wondering if he should have just stayed quiet and let the project fail on someone else's watch.

Most people in Michael's position fall into **Learned Helplessness** (Martin Seligman's term for passive resignation). They internalize the failure, believing they are powerless to change their circumstances. They become "present but absent," doing the bare minimum while sinking into depression. Alternatively, they burn the building down with **Toxic Reactivity**, sending angry emails, badmouthing the company, and destroying their own brand in a blaze of "justice."

Joseph did neither. He adopted a strategy of active waiting. He realized that while he could not control the location of his body, he remained the master of his attitude. He understood that his "internal state" was the only territory he still ruled.

Action Step: The Twenty-Four-Hour Rule & The Narrative Audit

If you have been unjustly accused or sidelined, you need a protocol to manage the trauma. Start with the **Twenty-Four-Hour Rule**. Give yourself permission to grieve for one full day. Feel the anger, write the letter you'll never send (and then delete it), scream in your car, or go for a run until your lungs burn. You must acknowledge the cortisol spike *because you cannot heal what you do not feel.* Repressing the emotion will only cause it to leak out later as bitterness.

After twenty-four hours, conduct a **Narrative Audit** to regain cognitive control. You must separate the raw event from the internal story. The event is simply that you were reassigned to a smaller role. The toxic story is telling yourself, "I am a failure, my career is over, and everyone hates me." You must replace this with an empowering story: "I am being protected from a sinking ship. I am now a consultant in exile. I have been given the gift of time to upskill. My character is being tested, and I will pass." Choosing the empowering narrative changes your biochemistry, prepares you for the next chapter, and shifts you from victim to student.

Leading When No One is Watching

The "Keeper of the Prison" Principle: Leading Without Authority

We look back at the text: *"But the Lord was with Joseph ... and He gave him favor in the sight of the keeper of the prison" (Genesis 39:21).*

This is a masterclass in **Influential Leadership** versus **Positional Leadership**. In traditional management theory, Positional Leadership (Level 1 in John Maxwell's model) relies on the title on your door, the budget you control, and the org chart. Influential Leadership (Level 2 and above) relies entirely on the content of your character and the value you add to others.

Joseph had no title. He was an inmate, stripped of all rights. He wore the rags of a prisoner. Yet, functionally, he ran the prison.

The text says, *"The keeper of the prison did not look into anything that was under Joseph's authority."* This implies that Joseph created a high-trust culture within a dungeon. He didn't just sit in the corner; he operationalized the chaos, turning a place of despair into a place of order. He likely organized the cleaning schedules in a closed underground silo where hygiene was a matter of life or death, perhaps taking the worst shifts himself to model the behavior. He managed the food distribution to ensure fairness and prevent riots among hungry men, creating systems of equity where there was only scarcity. He mediated disputes between violent political prisoners before they turned lethal, becoming the peacemaker in a war zone. He acted as the therapist, manager, and logistics officer, listening to the stories of men who had lost everything.

Ken Blanchard teaches that "Servant leadership is all about making the goals clear and then rolling your sleeves up." Joseph proved that you do not need permission to lead; you only need a towel and a willingness to solve problems that others ignore. He treated the prison as if it were his own business. He bloomed where he was planted, even though he was planted in sewage. He understood that **excellence is not a performance for the audience; it is a discipline for the soul.**

The Silent Creative

Consider **Tina**.

She is a brilliant UX designer for a major streaming platform. She possesses a rare combination of technical skill and deep empathy. She spends her weekends prototyping a revolutionary interface that would make the app 50% more accessible to the elderly and visually impaired. She presents it to her creative director with data, passion, and a working model.

He glances at it while checking his phone, sighs, and says, "It's nice, Tina, but it's not on the roadmap. We need to focus on monetization features, not charity. Stick to the ticket queue."

Six months later, the company is criticized in the press for poor accessibility. Tina's prototype sits on her hard drive, gathering digital dust. She feels the crushing weight of being "ahead of her time." She is in the Prison of Misunderstanding, the prison of unrecognized potential. She feels invisible, her expertise dismissed by someone with less vision but more authority. She watches as inferior ideas get funded simply because they are "safe."

The temptation for Tina is **Creative Retraction**. The natural human response is to do the bare minimum, to "quiet quit." She might think, "If they won't value my gold, I'll give them bronze. I will do exactly what they pay me for and nothing more. I will turn off my brain at 5:00 PM." This is a strategic error. It harms the company, yes, but more importantly, it atrophies her talent. It trains her to be mediocre. It dulls her blade. When the opportunity finally *does* come, she won't be ready because she has been practicing mediocrity.

But Joseph teaches us the **Principle of Steward-Ownership** and **Intrapreneurship**. You do not own your job; you own your *gift*. Joseph managed the prison with the same excellence he used to manage Potiphar's mansion, not because the prison deserved it, but because *excellence was his internal operating system*. He refused to let the environment lower his standard.

Tina must shift her mindset to a **Blue Ocean Strategy of the Soul**. Instead of competing for recognition in a crowded "Red Ocean" of office politics where she is currently losing, she creates a "Blue Ocean" of value where no one is looking. She builds a "Shadow Portfolio," continuing to refine the prototype not for the boss, but for the world she will one day serve, treating it as her master's thesis. She establishes thought leadership by writing white papers on accessibility standards and publishing them under her own name, becoming a voice in the industry that bypasses her boss entirely. She mentors the intern, passing on her knowledge and building a network of loyalty that transcends the hierarchy. She prepares for a future that hasn't arrived yet, realizing that her current employer is just an investor in her education.

Reflective Invitation: Ask yourself, are you withholding your best work because you aren't getting the credit? This is a trap. If you lower your output to match their appreciation, you become smaller. You allow their blindness to diminish your sight. Apply the litmus test: If you knew that your current obscurity was actually "training time" for a massive promotion in three years, how would you show up to work tomorrow? Would you sulk or would you sharpen your skills?

The Test of Time and the Trap of Politics

The Butler, The Baker, and The Stockdale Paradox

Genesis 40 introduces the politics of the palace, exported to the prison. The king's cupbearer (butler) and baker are thrown into Joseph's cell. These are high-value prisoners, privy to state secrets. The cupbearer was not just a waiter; he was the king's taste-tester and confidant. He controlled access to the throne. He was the gatekeeper.

Joseph notices their distress one morning. Note his **Emotional Intelligence (EQ)**: *"Why do you look so sad today?"* (Gen 40:7). This moment represents a profound shift. A man consumed by his own injustice doesn't notice the sadness of others. A victim asks, "Why does no one ask how *I* am doing?" but a leader asks, "How can I help you?" Joseph pivoted from *Self-Focus* to *Other-Focus*, refusing to let his own pain make him narcissistic. Even in the pit, he was serving.

He interprets their dreams. This was not a parlor trick; in Egyptian culture, dreams were considered messages from the gods. Interpreting them was a high-level diplomatic and theological skill. Joseph was practicing his gift in the dark, staying sharp for the moment he would need it. He delivers the news, good for the butler, fatal for the baker. And then, Joseph makes one request. A deeply human request: *"But remember me when it is well with you... make mention of me to Pharaoh."* (Gen 40:14)

The butler is restored. The plan works. And then comes the most painful verse in the chapter: *"Yet the chief cupbearer did not remember Joseph, but forgot him."* (Gen 40:23).

For two more years.

Here, Joseph embodies the **Stockdale Paradox**, named after Admiral Jim Stockdale, a POW in Vietnam. Stockdale survived eight years of torture by holding two contradictory beliefs simultaneously: the unwavering faith that he would prevail in the end, and the brutal discipline to face the facts of his current reality. The "optimists" in the prison camps died of broken hearts; they set deadlines like Christmas or Easter, and when those dates passed, they died. Joseph survived because he had faith in God's promise, yet he had the discipline to manage the prison day after day, year after year. He didn't live on false hope; he lived on grit. He accepted the reality of the delay without accepting the finality of the defeat. He woke up every morning for seven hundred thirty days knowing the Butler had forgotten him, and yet he still organized the prison.

Consider **Jordan.**

Jordan is a PhD candidate. He is diligent, meticulously researching data for the department's flagship study. He runs the stats, cleans the data, and writes the methodology. But Jordan is an introvert. He isn't good at the faculty cocktail parties. He struggles with small talk. He believes the work should speak for itself.

Then there is Seth. Seth is charming, loud, and politically savvy. Seth does 10% of the work but spends 90% of the time "managing up" to the Department Head. Seth knows whose laughter to echo and whose coffee to buy. Seth knows how to play the game.

When the grant money comes, and the publication is released, Seth is listed as the lead author. Jordan is buried in the footnotes. Seth gets the fellowship. Jordan gets more lab work. The faculty praise Alex's "leadership" and "vision," unaware that the vision was Jordan's. Jordan watches Seth rise on the elevator of politics while he takes the stairs of hard work. He is in the Round House, screaming internally, *It's not fair! I did the work! He just did the talking!* He feels the bitter taste of resentment, the feeling that the universe rewards the superficial and punishes the substantial. He considers quitting, leaking the data, or sabotaging the next phase.

The Law of the Lid vs. The Law of Solid Ground

John Maxwell teaches that trust is the foundation of leadership. In the short term, charisma (the butler/Seth) can get you a promotion. It acts as a lubricant for success. But character (Joseph/Jordan) is the foundation that keeps you there. The "Law of the Lid" states that leadership ability determines a person's level of effectiveness. Seth may have a high "Charisma Lid," but his "Character Lid" is low. Eventually, he will hit a ceiling he cannot talk his way through. When a crisis hits the department—a data audit, a funding freeze, a complex ethical dilemma—Seth will crumble because he lacks substance. Jordan will stand because he has roots.

The Butler represents **Transactional Networking**. He forgot Joseph because Joseph was no longer useful to him. That is how politics works; it is utilitarian. Jordan must realize he is in a **Season of Root Development**. Consider the Chinese Bamboo Tree. It spends five years developing underground root systems, showing no visible growth above ground. Then, in the fifth year, it shoots up eighty feet in six weeks. If Jordan quits now, he loses the root system. He must trust the **Law of Solid Ground**: character communicates consistency, potential, and respect.

When overshadowed by politics, use the **Reframing Triad** to maintain sanity. First, focus on competence. Politics can fake success, but it cannot fake competence forever. The market is ruthless; it eventually exposes the Seths of the world when they are required to deliver actual results during a crisis. Competence is the ultimate currency. Second, expand your network laterally. Do not rely on one "Butler." Diversify your relationships by building alliances with peers, not just patrons. Create a network that Seth cannot access because it is built on genuine service, not flattery. Finally, release the timeline. Stress occurs when your timeline (I should be promoted by now) clashes with God's timeline (You aren't ready for the weight of the crown yet). Trust the Architect of the process. The longer the preparation, the greater the assignment.

The Divine Perspective and Strategic Emergence

The Shave and The Change

We eventually reach Genesis 41. Pharaoh has a dream that terrifies him. The magicians are stumped. The Butler finally remembers the Hebrew in the dungeon. Joseph is summoned.

Notice the detail in verse 14: *"He shaved himself and changed his clothes, and came to Pharaoh."*

This is **Contextual Intelligence**. Hebrews were bearded; it was a sign of their masculinity and culture. Egyptians were fastidiously clean-shaven, often shaving their entire bodies to maintain purity and avoid lice in the heat. Joseph did not walk into the throne room asserting his rights or his cultural preference. He did not say, "Take me as I am. I've been wronged, and I demand justice." He realized the moment was not about him; it was about the solution he carried.

He adapted his presentation to remove barriers to his message. He understood the protocol of the court. He utilized **Code**

Switching—the ability to adjust one's style of speech, appearance, and behavior to optimize comfort for others in exchange for fair consideration. He was ready to speak the language of power. He showed respect for the office of Pharaoh even before he met the man. This wasn't a compromise; it was wisdom. It was the ability to read the room before he even entered it, removing every distraction so that the king could focus on the message, not the messenger's appearance.

God Meant It For Good: The Ultimate Strategic Alignment

He interprets the dream. He offers a strategic plan (store 20% of the grain during the boom years to survive the bust years). And in an instant, he is elevated from Prisoner #42 to Prime Minister.

But here is the critical insight: **Joseph could not have saved Egypt if he had not been in prison.** The prison was not dead time after all.

In Potiphar's house, he learned micro-economics, managing a high-net-worth household, supply chains, and personnel on a small scale. In the Prison, he learned macro-politics by dealing with the king's prisoners, the political elite. He learned the dark underbelly of the Egyptian legal system and heard the secrets of the court from the butler and baker. He learned how the palace *really* worked. He mastered crisis management, learning how to handle diverse personalities, manage scarce resources during a shortage, and maintain order in a volatile environment. Most importantly, his character was forged. He learned that his gift was not for his own glory, but for the saving of many lives. The arrogance of the "dreamer" who bragged to his brothers was gone; the humility of the servant remained.

If Michael (The Scapegoat) eventually starts his own consulting firm because he was pushed out, the prison was a strategic pivot that forced him to leave a comfort zone. If Tina (The Creative) eventually becomes the Chief Product Officer because she spent the quiet years mastering her craft, the silence was essential R&D time. If Jordan (The Student) eventually leads a research institute based on integrity, the oversight was a character test that saved him from becoming a shallow academic like Seth.

This brings us to the ultimate cognitive reframe, found later in Genesis 50:20: *"But as for you, you meant evil against me; but God meant it for good."*

This is **Providential Strategy**. It is the ability to look at the wreckage of your reputation, the injustice of your reassignment, and the silence of your phone, and say: *"This is raw material. God is building a leader. The enemy intended to bury me, but he didn't know I was a seed."* It is the theological conviction that God wastes nothing—not your pain, not your tears, and not your time in the dark.

My Reflection

My fellow leaders, I do not know what number is on your prison uniform today.

I do not know if you are staring at a termination letter, a rejection email, or a blank wall of silence. I do not know if you are Michael, quietly packing his box; Tina, closing her laptop in frustration; or Jordan, looking at a paper that bears someone else's name.

But I know this: **The pit is not your potential. The prison is not your residence. It is your classroom.**

Do not waste this pain. Do not spend this season shaking the bars and screaming at the guards. That only exhausts you. Instead, turn around. Look at the prisoners next to you. Serve them. Lead them. Organize the dungeon. Sharpen your gift.

The butler may forget you. The VP may blame you. The professor may ignore you. But the Creator has not taken His eye off you.

You are being forged. You are being tempered. The heat is high because the calling is great.

Hold the line. Keep the faith. And when the door finally opens—and it *will* open—you will not walk out as a bitter victim, smelling of the dungeon. You will walk out as a ruler prepared to save the very world that rejected you.

Stand up. Shake off the dust. Your season is coming.

The Prisoner's Inventory

Read Genesis 41:14. Note that before Joseph went to Pharaoh, he "shaved and changed his clothes." He had to shed the identity of the victim to step into the identity of the victor.

- **Question:** If you were called to the Palace today, are you ready? Or are you still wearing the "garments" of a prisoner (bitterness, victimhood, cynicism, gossip)?
- **Action:** Identify one "prisoner garment" you need to take off today. Write it down. Throw it away. Prepare for the summons.

If you are navigating a high-stakes transition and want to apply this framework to your own situation with clarity and discipline, scan the QR code below for a Transition Readiness Chat.

CHAPTER 6

The Discipline of Solitude: Building Creative Capacity in Hidden Seasons

"In solitude the mind gains strength and learns to lean upon itself."

— Laurence Sterne

If you were to engineer the perfect environment for the systematic destruction of a human soul, you would likely build an Ancient Egyptian dungeon.

To truly understand the weight of Joseph's ordeal, we must strip away the sanitized Sunday School visuals of a tidy room with a barred window and a straw mat. Archaeological evidence and linguistic clues in the Hebrew text paint a far more terrifying picture. The Hebrew word used for Joseph's prison is *sohar*, a term that is linguistically unique and often translated as "Round House" or fortress. However, rigorous Egyptological studies suggest these were not merely holding cells in the modern sense. They were subterranean silos, massive, hollowed-out granaries or cisterns repurposed for human containment.

These were voids. They were sensory deprivation tanks designed to strip a man of his identity, his agency, and his future. The architecture was designed to break the will. Often shaped like a flask, with a narrow neck at the top for air and food, the body of the prison widened underground, making escape physically impossible without assistance from above. The air was stagnant, heavy with the dust of the Nile delta, the scent of unwashed bodies, and the crushing weight of despair. There was no natural light to track the sun, no clock to mark the passing of time, and no stimulation to keep the mind tethered to reality.

They were dark, damp, and silent—the kind of silence that doesn't bring peace, but madness. In the Ancient Near East, to be cast into the pit was to be treated as if you were already dead—removed from the land of the living, forgotten by the gods, and erased from the social register. You were a non-entity, swallowed by the earth. For an Egyptian, whose entire theology revolved around the sun and visibility, this darkness was not just imprisonment; it was a spiritual nullification. To be unseen was to cease to exist.

And yet, it was here, not in the coat of many colors that marked his father's favor, and not in the opulent halls of Potiphar where he managed wealth, that Joseph became the man who would save civilization.

We often look at the "wilderness seasons" of our lives as lost time. It might be unemployment, bankruptcy, isolation, the failure of a startup, or the quiet years of obscurity. We treat them like waiting rooms, pacing back and forth, reading old magazines, checking our watches, and begging God to call our number so we can get back to "real life." We view silence as an enemy to be defeated with noise, podcasts, streaming services, and constant activity. We are terrified of the quiet because we are terrified of what we might hear when the noise stops. We fill every gap in our schedule because we equate busyness with significance.

But what if we have it all wrong? What if the darkness isn't a delay? What if the darkness is a darkroom?

In the study of leadership and neurobiology, there is a concept known as incubation. It is the phenomenon where the brain, removed from the noise of constant input, engages the Default Mode Network. In our hyper-connected world, our brains are constantly in executive function mode, processing to-do lists, reacting to notifications, and navigating social dynamics. But neuroscience shows that innovation rarely happens in this state. It is only when the noise stops—when we enter the dungeon of solitude—that the executive function quiets down and the subconscious takes over.

This is the neural network responsible for daydreaming, envisioning the future, and consolidating memories. It is where the mind connects disparate dots, where linear logic gives way to lateral genius, and where raw data becomes wisdom. It is the birthplace of the "aha!" moment, characterized by a sudden burst of high-frequency gamma waves in the brain. It is in the darkroom that the image, captured in a split second of inspiration, is slowly developed into a permanent picture.

Joseph entered the prison a favored son with a dream, a somewhat naive boy who thought the world revolved around his sheaf of wheat bowing down to him. He left the prison a strategic genius with a comprehensive plan to feed the known world. The transformation didn't happen in the light of public praise. It happened in the dark of private processing.

This chapter is about reclaiming your wilderness. It is about understanding that solitude is not a sentence; it is a strategy. Whether you are an entrepreneur building a prototype in a basement because you can't afford an office, a writer staring at a blank page in a season of grief, or a leader stripped of your title and influence, you are standing on holy ground. You are not in a tomb. You are in an incubator.

The Architecture of Isolation

State Management in the Cell

Let's get real about the brutality of Joseph's situation. He has been betrayed by his brothers, sold as a commodity, trafficked across borders, falsely accused of sexual assault, and thrown into a hole in the ground. From a psychological standpoint, Joseph was a prime candidate for complex post-traumatic stress disorder. The compounding layers of trauma—betrayal, loss of autonomy, and unjust imprisonment—created a perfect storm for cognitive collapse. Psychological studies on prisoners of war and long-term inmates show that the loss of autonomy is the single greatest predictor of mental decline.

Most people in this scenario react in one of two ways. They either dissociate, checking out mentally and succumbing to the victim identity known as learned helplessness, or they rage, burning up their limited emotional energy screaming at the walls, consumed by bitterness. This state creates a toxic internal chemical bath of cortisol and adrenaline that destroys the body. It is a metabolic burn rate that no human can sustain for a decade.

Joseph did neither. He mastered what Tony Robbins calls state management, and what psychologists like Viktor Frankl refer to as the "last of the human freedoms." In his seminal work *Man's Search for Meaning*, Frankl, writing from the abyss of a Nazi concentration camp, argued that while everything can be taken from a man—his status, his clothes, his health—the last of the human freedoms is to choose one's attitude in any given set of circumstances. He called this the will to meaning. Joseph realized that while he could not control the location of his body, he could absolutely control the focus of his mind.

The Bible gives us a fascinating detail in Genesis 39:22, noting that the keeper of the prison put all the prisoners under Joseph's authority. Joseph didn't have a title or freedom; he wore chains.

Yet, he took ownership of the environment that enslaved him. He essentially became the CEO of the dungeon, managing food distribution, sanitation, and dispute resolution.

Think about the operational reality of this. He had to manage the egos of dangerous men, allocate scarce resources fairly to prevent riots, and maintain hygiene in a subterranean pit. He turned a place of death into a place of function. He imposed order on chaos, not because he was asked to, but because his internal identity was that of a ruler, regardless of his external address. He was practicing governance in a simulator. He was learning how to lead men who had nothing to lose—the hardest kind of leadership there is.

We see this dynamic mirrored in the life of Nelson Mandela. Imprisoned for twenty-seven years, Mandela did not merely "serve time." He transformed Robben Island into a university. While working in the blinding limestone quarries, he and his fellow prisoners organized political debates, educated younger prisoners in history and economics, and even learned the Afrikaans language of their oppressors to better understand them. Mandela famously stated, "I was not a messiah, but an ordinary man who had become a leader because of extraordinary circumstances." Like Joseph, *he managed his state before he managed a nation.* He realized that if he let the prison define him, he would leave as a bitter man, not a leader. The cell was his classroom; the guards were his study subjects.

Modern creativity research, particularly the work done on the constraints principle, suggests that unbridled freedom often kills innovation. When we have infinite resources, infinite time, and infinite options, we tend to follow the path of least resistance. We bloat. We stagnate. We throw money at problems rather than intellect. But place a human being in a box—limit their resources, restrict their movement—and the brain kicks into survival mode. It becomes hyper-efficient. It scans for patterns it would otherwise miss. This is known as cognitive surplus—where the mental energy usually spent on navigating choices is redirected toward solving a singular, pressing problem.

Consider the story of Steve Jobs in his "wilderness years" after being fired from Apple in 1985. He was stripped of the company he built and humiliated publicly. The press wrote him off as a one-hit wonder. Yet, in that isolation, he didn't just wait. He founded NeXT and bought a small, struggling graphics division called Pixar. Without the infinite resources of Apple, he was forced to learn the architecture of a different kind of computer and the art of storytelling. He had to grind. It wasn't an overnight success; it was years of failure and iteration. But when he returned to Apple over a decade later, he wasn't just a tech guy; he was a storyteller who understood hardware. The wilderness gave him the tools to rebuild the empire. The iPod did not come from the twenty-year-old Jobs; it came from the man who had been humbled and honed in the desert.

The Leadership Axiom:

You cannot lead on the throne if you haven't led in the dungeon. If you can't create order in a 10x10 cell, you cannot create order in a kingdom. The dungeon is the simulator for the sovereign.

The Alchemy of Interpretation

The Blanchard Principle: Servant Leadership as a Discovery Tool

Two years into his imprisonment, Joseph encounters the cupbearer and the baker. Historically, we minimize these roles, imagining a waiter and a cook. This is a mistake. In the Egyptian court, these were high-ranking cabinet officials. The cupbearer was the head of security and the most trusted confidant of the Pharaoh—the one man whose loyalty had to be absolute, as he literally held the king's life in his hands. The baker controlled the entire food supply chain for the palace, a role of immense logistical importance.

Joseph was managing disgraced executives. He was in a masterclass of Egyptian politics, listening to the gossip, the fears, and the structural failures of the palace from the men who ran it. He was gathering intelligence on how the empire worked, even while wearing shackles. He was learning the org chart of the nation he was destined to lead.

Here is the pivotal moment. It is morning. Joseph walks in to attend to them and notices they are sad. This is the key to innovation: observation born of empathy. Ken Blanchard often teaches that leadership is not about being served, but about serving. In the context of creativity, service is the ultimate unlock code because empathy is the engine of problem-solving. You cannot solve a problem you do not understand, and you cannot understand a problem if you are obsessed with yourself. Most prisoners are narcissists by necessity—survival focuses the mind inward on one's own hunger, fear, and discomfort.

But Joseph broke this pattern. He noticed the micro-expressions on their faces. He stopped his own routine to ask a question: *"Why do you look so sad today?"*

That question changed history. It required him to look past his own iron shackles to see the emotional shackles of another. It required him to suspend his own agenda—his own desire to scream "I am innocent!"—to attend to their anxiety.

When the prisoners told their dreams, Joseph utilized a gift that had been sharpened by silence. He listened. In the quiet of the prison, Joseph had learned to listen to God and to observe human nature. He connected the spiritual reality to the physical evidence. He saw the symbolism of "lifting up the head" in two very different ways. For the cupbearer, the three branches represented three days until restoration, a lifting of the head to honor. For the baker, the three baskets represented three days until execution—a lifting of the head *from* the body. This wasn't a guess; it was an interpretation derived from spiritual intimacy and keen observation. Joseph risked his reputation by delivering the hard truth to the baker, demonstrating that true leadership speaks truth even when it is painful.

Think of the engineer who is laid off. In the panic of unemployment, many freeze. But the "Josephs" of the modern era look around at the pain of others. Take the example of Brian Chesky and Joe Gebbia. During the 2008 recession, they were broke and unemployed in San Francisco. They were designers with no money and rent due. Instead of looking inward at their own poverty, they looked outward and saw a problem: hotels were booked solid for a design conference, and travelers had nowhere to stay. They realized there was a "sadness" in the market, a lack of connection and affordable housing.

They didn't have resources, but they had an air mattress. They solved a problem for others to solve their own problem. But it wasn't easy. They funded their early days by creating novelty cereal boxes—"Obama O's" and "Cap'n McCain's"—gluing the boxes together with hot glue guns in their kitchen. They sold them for $40 a box to keep the lights on. Airbnb was born in the "dungeon" of scarcity because two men decided to interpret the needs of strangers rather than dwell on their own lack. They saw a resource (empty living rooms) where everyone else saw nothing.

Joseph's creativity wasn't just "having a good idea." It was an interpretation. It was taking the raw, confusing data of someone else's life and offering clarity. Innovation is rarely creating something from nothing; it is usually bringing order to chaos and meaning to confusion.

The Wilderness of the Mind

The Maxwell Principle: The Law of Process

Joseph interpreted the dream correctly. The cupbearer was restored. And then comes the most painful verse in the story: *"Yet the chief cupbearer did not remember Joseph, but forgot him."*

Two more years passed.

This is the "Gap." It is the space between the promise and the payoff. John Maxwell teaches the Law of Process: leadership develops daily, not in a day. If Joseph had been released the moment he interpreted the dream, he would have been a free man, but he would not have been a ruler. He wasn't ready. He had the gift of interpretation, but he didn't yet have the character of endurance. He had the flash of insight, but not the steadiness of command.

Neuroscientists talk about the difference between procedural memory (the "how-to" of riding a bike) and declarative memory (facts and figures). But there is a third kind of deep learning that only happens over time: *wisdom consolidation*. This is the slow-cooking process where experiences, failures, and observations are integrated into the personality. During those two silent years, Joseph was moving from talent to authority. Talent dazzles, but authority sustains. Talent opens the door, but character keeps you in the room. The two years of silence were not God ignoring Joseph; they were God thickening his shoulders so he could bear the weight of the coat that was coming. God was shifting Joseph's identity from a "man with a gift" to a "man of God." He had to learn how to deal with "hope deferred," which makes the heart sick (Proverbs 13:12), without becoming sick in his soul.

This period exemplifies what Jim Collins calls the Stockdale Paradox, named after Admiral James Stockdale, who was a prisoner of war in Vietnam for seven years. When asked who didn't make it out of the camps, Stockdale replied, "The optimists." The ones who said, "We'll be out by Christmas." Christmas would come and go. Then Easter. Then Thanksgiving. Eventually, they died of a broken heart. Stockdale survived because he embraced two opposing realities simultaneously. He retained absolute faith that he would prevail in the end, regardless of the difficulties, while simultaneously confronting the most brutal facts of his current reality, whatever they might be. Joseph had the faith of his dreams but had to confront the brutal fact of the cupbearer's forgetfulness. He didn't break; he consolidated. He managed the prison one day at a time, keeping his skills sharp and his spirit ready.

J.K. Rowling wrote the early drafts of *Harry Potter* while on welfare, a single mother, struggling with clinical depression. She was "forgotten" by society, a statistical failure in the eyes of the British economy. But in that silence, she built a world. She didn't just write a story; she constructed a universe with rules, depth, histories, and internal logic. She later said that rock bottom became the solid foundation on which she rebuilt her life. If she had been "discovered" after the first chapter, the depth of the series might never have materialized. The wilderness gave her the time to build the architecture of the story.

Similarly, John Bunyan wrote *The Pilgrim's Progress*—one of the most significant works of English literature—while imprisoned in Bedford Gaol for twelve years for preaching without a license. The constraint of the prison walls forced his imagination to expand into a spiritual journey that has guided millions. He mapped the geography of the soul because he could not travel the geography of the earth.

If you are in a season where you feel forgotten, you are likely in the Inventory Phase. You are stocking the shelves of your soul. You are gathering the raw materials—patience, humility, resilience, and specific knowledge—that you will need when the doors open. Do not despise the silence; it is the sound of your foundation being poured.

The Synthesis: Preparation Meets Opportunity

The call finally comes. Pharaoh has a dream. The experts, the magicians and wise men of Egypt, are stumped. They had the data, the charts, and the books, but they lacked the insight. They were technically proficient but spiritually blind. The Cupbearer remembers his fault, and Joseph is shaved, changed, and brought before the most powerful man on earth.

Here is where the "Creativity Born in Darkness" manifests. Pharaoh tells the dream (fat cows, skinny cows). Joseph does two things. First, he offers the spiritual interpretation: "God has shown Pharaoh what He is about to do." He gives the credit to God, maintaining his integrity even before the king.

Second, and most critically, he executes a strategic pivot. This is the part we miss. Joseph didn't stop at the interpretation. A mere prophet would have delivered the message and left. A leader steps into the gap.

Genesis 41:33: *"Now therefore, let Pharaoh select a discerning and wise man, and set him over the land of Egypt. Let Pharaoh do this, and let him appoint officers over the land, to collect one-fifth of the produce..."*

Wait a minute. Pharaoh asked for an interpretation. He didn't ask for a business plan. He didn't ask for a McKinsey consultant to restructure the agricultural economy of the Nile.

But Joseph had spent roughly thirteen years in the "school of darkness." He understood logistics (from running Potiphar's estate). He understood human nature and crime (from the prison). He understood resource allocation. He saw the gap between the vision (famine) and the reality (survival). He realized that revelation without application is hallucination.

Ronald Heifetz distinguishes between technical challenges (problems with known solutions) and adaptive challenges (problems requiring new learning and systemic change). The famine was an adaptive challenge that threatened the existence of the empire. Joseph offered a policy framework that fundamentally shifted the Egyptian economy from a decentralized feudal system to a centralized theocratic state.

First, he proposed a fiscal policy based on a 20% flat tax (one-fifth) during the boom years. This is classic counter-cyclical economics, saving the surplus of the good years to stimulate the economy in the lean years. Note the wisdom here: he didn't confiscate 50% or 100%. He left 80% with the people to incentivize production, but he taxed the 20% surplus that would otherwise be wasted. He knew human nature would be to consume the surplus, so he mandated savings, creating what was arguably the first sovereign wealth fund in history.

Next, he revolutionized supply chain logistics through centralized storage. This required massive infrastructure projects, creating jobs and ensuring food security. He had to design silos that could preserve grain for seven years without spoilage from moisture, pests, or theft. This was a massive engineering feat. He likely applied the knowledge of the "silos" he had been imprisoned in, using the architecture of the pit to save the people. He turned the instrument of his captivity into the instrument of their salvation.

Finally, he established a clear organizational hierarchy. He advised Pharaoh to "appoint officers," knowing that a flat structure would fail under the pressure of famine. He built a chain of command to execute the collection and distribution, creating a meritocratic bureaucracy that could outlast the crisis.

Many Christians are great at the vision, but they fail at the venture. They can describe the problem, but they cannot design the solution. The time in the darkness is designed to teach you the mechanics of reality so that when the vision comes, you know how to build the container for it. Joseph proved that true spirituality is not just hearing God; it is applying God's wisdom to the practical problems of the world.

The Call to Creative Command

We are living in a world that is desperate for interpretation. Our economies are volatile, our culture is fractured, and our leaders are confused. They are dreaming disturbing dreams and waking up trembling. The old playbooks are failing, and the magicians of our age—the economists, the pundits, the politicians—are standing silent before the problem.

They don't need more noise. They don't need more panic. They don't need more people pointing out how dark it is.

They need "Josephs."

They need men and women who have done their time in the darkroom. People who have mastered their state when life was unfair, served the sad when they were hurting themselves, and endured the delay without losing their faith.

Stop looking at your current struggle as a grave. It is not a grave. It is a mine. Dig deep. The gold of your future authority is buried in the rock of your current suffering.

If you are in the basement, build. If you are in the wilderness, write. If you are in prison, lead.

The palace is not the goal. The goal is to become the kind of person who can save many lives (Genesis 50:20) when the famine comes. The darkness is your friend. Embrace it, interpret it, and prepare to speak when the king calls.

The Discipline of Darkness

To apply these principles, we must first address our physiology, as it dictates our psychology. Tony Robbins teaches that when we feel the crushing weight of circumstances, we often slump or hide.

The challenge is to stand up and change our state. If you can't control your career right now, control your body. Go for a run, pray with volume, and disrupt the pattern of despair. Start every morning with movement before looking at your phone to train your body to lead your mind.

Secondly, we must adopt the service scan. Servant leadership is the cure for isolation. Identify the "cupbearer" in your life right now—the person with a minor problem that you have the major skill to solve. Perform one unasked act of kindness for a colleague, neighbor, or family member this week without asking for credit; just interpret their need and fill it.

Finally, we must enact a preparation plan. Remember John Maxwell's Law of the Lid—your current skills will not sustain your future dream. Identify the specific technical skill missing from your toolbox, whether it be financial literacy, public speaking, or theology, and dedicate time every day in your "prison" to mastering it. Treat your downtime not as a punishment, but as a university.

If you are navigating a high-stakes transition and want to apply this framework to your own situation with clarity and discipline, scan the QR code below for a Transition Readiness Chat.

CHAPTER 7

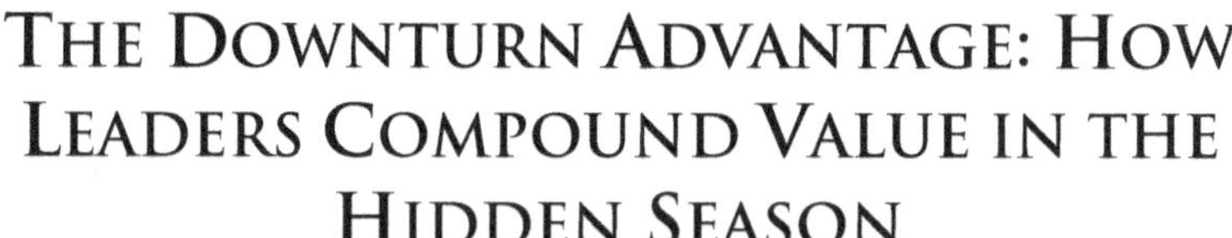

The Downturn Advantage: How Leaders Compound Value in the Hidden Season

"When we are no longer able to change a situation, we are challenged to change ourselves."

— Viktor E. Frankl

The Economics of the Pit

If you analyze the life of Joseph through a purely secular, modern lens, his resume appears to be a catastrophic failure for the first thirteen years of his adult life. He is the victim of human trafficking, sold by his own blood relatives for twenty shekels of silver—the price of a wounded slave, a discount on a human soul. He is falsely accused of sexual assault by a powerful woman whose word is law, a charge that carries the weight of a capital offense. He is an inmate in an Egyptian dungeon, a place of darkness and despair, forgotten by the very people he helped. By every external metric like status, income, visibility, social capital, and career trajectory, Joseph is in a severe, unrecoverable recession. He has been stripped of his name, his rights, his geography, and his future.

But if you look at Joseph through the lens of **Strategic Self-Investment**, those thirteen years were not a recession; they were the most aggressive period of capital accumulation in human history.

Most people view a "hidden season"—a sudden job loss, a painful divorce, a lingering sickness, a demotion, or a quiet, stagnant period in ministry—as "dead time." It feels like a pause button has been hit on your life while everyone else is in fast-forward. You watch peers get promoted, friends get married, and competitors gain market share while you seem to be standing still, trapped in amber. Psychologically, the brain often interprets this lack of external validation as rejection or abandonment. It triggers a limbic system "freeze response," flooding the body with cortisol and leading to apathy, depression, or a desperate, frantic scrambling for attention. You see this season as a waiting room where you sit, read old magazines, and hope your name gets called. You believe the pernicious lie that your value is on hold until the spotlight returns.

That is a lie that will bankrupt your destiny.

The Hidden Season is not a waiting room; it is a classroom. It is an incubator. It is the darkroom where the image of your future impact is developed. Without the dark, there is no definition. A seed that is buried looks like it is dead, but it is actually undergoing the most violent and critical transformation of its life. It is shedding its shell to break open new life. The pressure of the soil is not there to crush the seed, but to crack it open. If you dig up the seed to check on it, you kill the process. You must trust the darkness.

In this chapter, we are going to dismantle the passive approach to suffering. We are adopting a new thesis: **The quality of your public revelation is determined by the intensity of your private preparation.** We will walk through the Joseph narrative not just as a Sunday School story, but as a blueprint for high-performance leadership development. We will blend the fire of personal mastery, the insights of behavioral psychology, the grit of archeological history, and the calm assurance of spiritual formation to prove that your "pit" is actually your launchpad.

You are not buried; you are planted, and it is time to grow.

The Thesis of Self-Reinvestment

Tony Robbins often talks about the "State of Mind" and the power of physiology and focus—how we can change our internal state in an instant, regardless of external chaos. John Maxwell talks about the "Law of Process"—that leaders develop daily, not in a day. Ken Blanchard speaks to the "Heart of a Leader" and the necessity of servant leadership. Joseph embodies all three, demonstrating a profound shift in what psychologists call **Locus of Control**.

When Joseph was thrown into the pit by his brothers and later sold to Potiphar, he lost his coat—the symbol of his father's favor, his inheritance, and his unique identity. He lost his freedom. He lost his language and his culture. Yet, he refused to adopt an "External Locus of Control"—the belief that outside forces (brothers, Potiphar, Pharaoh, the economy) dictate his reality. A person with an external locus of control becomes a professional victim, constantly waiting for the environment to change so they can feel better. They outsource their emotional stability to the whims of their oppressors, becoming a thermometer that merely reflects the temperature of the room.

Instead, Joseph shifted to an "Internal Locus of Control." He realized he couldn't control the macro-events; he couldn't stop the slave caravan, silence the lies of Potiphar's wife, or speed up the slow wheels of the Egyptian justice system. But he could rigorously control his micro-responses. He could control his work ethic, his integrity, his attitude, and his connection to God. He understood that while he was not the master of his fate in a legal sense, he was the captain of his soul in a spiritual sense. He became a thermostat, setting the temperature of the environment he was placed in.

This shift is critical because **passive waiting is distinct from active preparation.** The victim asks, "Why is this happening to me?" The investor asks, "What can I extract from this?" Joseph extracted value from the pit.

True Capital is not what you have in your pocket; it is what you have in your mind and your spirit.

The thesis of Self-Reinvestment posits that when external resources are stripped away, you must double down on internal resource generation. You cannot control the market, the pharaohs, or the false accusers. You *can* control your skill acquisition, your emotional regulation, and your spiritual depth. When the external world says "stop," the internal world must say "build." The goal is not merely to survive the season, but to outgrow it, to become so large on the inside that the prison can no longer contain you.

The Three Currencies of the Hidden Season

During his time in Potiphar's house and the prison, Joseph aggressively accumulated three distinct types of currency that would later buy his success in the palace. These are currencies that inflation cannot devalue and thieves cannot steal.

First, he built **Intellectual Capital**. He didn't just sweep floors; he mastered administrative skills, cross-cultural literacy, logistics, and management. He learned how the Egyptian economy worked from the ground up, understanding the flow of goods, people, and power. He studied the language of his captors until he could speak it better than they could, understanding their idioms and humor. He moved from unskilled labor to executive management within the confines of his captivity, learning the physics of the Nile and the math of the harvest.

Simultaneously, he deepened his **Spiritual Capital**. He developed a robust theology of suffering, learning that God's presence isn't limited to the sanctuary of his father's tent. He cultivated a reliance on God's presence that was independent of his circumstances and a prophetic sensitivity that could not be shaken by betrayal. He moved from a faith inherited from Jacob to a faith forged in the fire of personal experience. He learned that God's silence is not God's absence, but often His attentive observation.

Finally, he expanded his relational capital. He honed his emotional intelligence, conflict resolution skills, and ability to build trust in hostile environments. He learned to read people, to serve those who could give him nothing in return, and to maintain his dignity when treated like property. He learned how to manage up toward Potiphar, manage down toward the prisoners, and manage across toward the cupbearer. He built a network of trust in a place designed for distrust.

Reflective Invitation: *Where are you feeling "stripped" right now? If you stopped viewing this loss as a deficit and started viewing it as space for investment, what would change in your daily schedule? Are you spending your energy trying to escape the pit, or are you furnishing it?*

Intellectual Capital (Education & Skills)

"So Joseph found favor in his sight and attended him, and he made him overseer of his house and put him in charge of all that he had."
— Genesis 39:4

Let's get practical. How does a shepherd boy from Canaan—a nomad with no formal education, no connections, and a criminal record—become the Prime Minister of Egypt, the greatest superpower of the ancient world? It wasn't a miracle download. God didn't zap Joseph with knowledge of Egyptian tax law, geometry, or agricultural science while he was sleeping.

Joseph learned it. He engaged in what Anders Ericsson calls "Deliberate Practice." He treated his slavery not as a sentence, but as an apprenticeship. He viewed Potiphar's house not as a place of servitude, but as a graduate school of management.

From a neurological perspective, active learning is the antidote to the "learned helplessness" often found in trauma survivors. When humans are subjected to uncontrollable stressors, the brain tends to shut down the prefrontal cortex (the center of planning and logic) and operate from the amygdala (the survival center). This leads to passivity and a "victim" mentality. When Joseph arrived in Potiphar's house, he fought this biology. He leveraged neuroplasticity—the brain's ability to reorganize itself by forming new neural connections. He forced his brain to adapt, to learn, and to master a foreign environment. By engaging in complex cognitive tasks, he kept his executive function sharp, preventing the trauma from atrophying his mind.

The Complexity of the Task

We must understand what it meant to be an "overseer" in Ancient Egypt during the Middle Kingdom. Archeology reveals that large Egyptian estates were complex, multi-faceted economic engines that functioned like modern corporations.

The role demanded scribal literacy and bureaucracy. Joseph likely had to master the Hieratic script—the cursive form of hieroglyphs used for administration—to read ledgers, inventory lists, and legal correspondence. Egypt was a bureaucracy run on papyrus; you could not lead if you could not read. He had to learn the difference between royal decrees and local ordinances.

It also required advanced supply chain management. Egyptian estates were self-contained cities managing grain silos, livestock herds, textile production, bakeries, breweries, and trade on the Nile. Joseph had to understand the agricultural calendar, the flooding cycles of the Nile (the *Inundation*), and the mathematics of storage and spoilage. He had to calculate yields, manage labor forces, and predict shortages.

Later, in the "Great Prison" (likely at Thebes or a royal confinement center), Joseph wasn't just a jailer; he was an administrator of state enemies. He managed intake, disputes, and the daily welfare of high-profile inmates, including the king's cupbearer. This gave him insight into court politics, royal protocol, and palace intrigues before he ever set foot in it. He learned the secrets of the state from the men who had fallen from its grace.

He didn't sulk; he studied. He mastered the logistics of a wealthy estate and the penal system of a superpower. **He was overqualified for his crisis.** By the time he stood before Pharaoh, he didn't just have a dream interpretation; he had an MBA in Egyptian Economics earned in the trenches of servitude.

Consider **Star**, a marketing executive laid off during a corporate merger.

For three months, the phone didn't ring. The "Waiting Room" mindset says: *Netflix, scroll LinkedIn, and panic.* This is the limbic system hijacking the brain, keeping her in a state of fight-or-flight, where creativity dies and anxiety rules. She feels the atrophy of her skills and the erosion of her confidence.

The "Joseph Mindset" says: *Strategic Self-Investment.* Star engages her prefrontal cortex—the center of executive function and planning. She refuses to let her employment status dictate her work ethic. She decides that her "job" is now self-improvement.

Star looked at the market trends and realized the industry was pivoting to AI-driven data analytics, an area where she was weak. She didn't just apply for jobs; she treated her unemployment as a full-time university. She structured her day with military precision. Her mornings, from 7:00 AM to 9:00 AM, were dedicated to spiritual discipline, anchoring her identity so rejection wouldn't stick. She started the day with gratitude, not desperation, visualizing her future success to prime her **Reticular Activating System (RAS)** to spot opportunities.

The midday block, from 9:00 AM to 1:00 PM, became her deep work session. She engaged in certification coursework for data analytics, Python, and prompt engineering, treating this time with the same rigidity as a client meeting. She turned off her phone and entered a state of flow. Her afternoons, from 2:00 PM to 4:00 PM, were reserved for strategic networking. She focused on building "cupbearer" connections, offering value by sending articles and insights rather than just asking for favors. She acted like a connector, even when she was disconnected.

Six months later, Star didn't just re-enter the market; she re-entered at a tier higher than she left. She was "ten times stronger" because she converted her grief into grit and her downtime into uptime. She didn't wait for the opportunity; she prepared for it.

The Lesson: The marketplace pays for value, not for your pity story. Use the hidden season to sharpen the axe. When the tree finally presents itself, you won't need twenty swings; you'll only need one.

Action Step: Identify one "hard skill" that is currently missing from your leadership toolkit—is it financial modeling, public speaking, a new software, or a second language? Commit thirty minutes a day for the next 90 days to master it. No excuses.

Spiritual Capital (The Discipline of the Soul)

Ken Blanchard reminds us that "Leadership is an inside job." You cannot lead others further than you have led yourself. If your internal foundation is weak, external pressure will crack you. The higher the building, the deeper the foundation must be.

Joseph's most significant threat wasn't Potiphar's wife or the prison guards; it was bitterness. He had every right to be toxic. His brothers tried to kill him. His boss threw him in jail for doing the right thing. The cupbearer, whom he served faithfully, forgot him for two years. This is the recipe for a hardened heart and a cynical spirit.

If Joseph had not invested in **Emotional Healing** and **Spiritual Discipline**, the palace would have destroyed him. Psychology tells us that unhealed trauma seeks repetition. A bitter man given absolute power becomes a tyrant (seeking revenge on the world for his pain). A healed man given absolute power becomes a savior.

The Ministry of the Dungeon: Post-Traumatic Growth

Joseph's spiritual formation didn't happen in the temple; it happened in the trauma. He exemplifies **Post-Traumatic Growth (PTG)**—the psychological theory that people can experience positive life changes *as a result* of their struggle with a major crisis. This isn't just "bouncing back" (resilience); it is "bouncing forward" (growth). It involves a radical restructuring of one's worldview.

He practiced the Presence. "The Lord was with Joseph" is the refrain of Genesis 39. Joseph learned to find God without the props of his father's religion—no altar, no sacrifice, no family gathering, no prophetic coat. He learned that God was portable. He discovered that the presence of God was not tied to a geography (Canaan) but to a heart posture. He learned to worship in the dark.

He also practiced **Cognitive Reframing**. This is the ability to identify and dispute irrational or maladaptive thoughts. You don't name your firstborn Manasseh ("God has made me forget all my hardship") without doing deep shadow work. He consciously chose to reframe his history not as a tragedy of victimization, but as a necessary, providential path to his destiny. He decided that the pain was a tool, not a weapon used against him. He viewed his suffering not as God's absence, but as God's hidden chisel.

Consider **Ronald.**

Meet **Ronald**, a pastor burning out from twenty years of service. He was cynical, tired, and spiritually dry. The congregation saw a leader; his family saw a ghost. The board mandated a sabbatical. Ron could have just slept for three months or played golf. But he chose *Strategic Self-Investment.*

He went to a monastery to break the addiction to noise. He unplugged from social media (the noise of the marketplace) to detox his dopamine receptors. He engaged a clinical therapist to deal with childhood wounds he had masked with ministry success—the "performance trap" that said he was only loved if he was preaching or producing. He read theology not to preach it, but to eat it. He learned to be a son before he was a servant.

He returned not just rested, but *renovated.* He had moved from doing things *for* God (transactional) to doing things *with* God (relational). He realized that his ministry was an overflow of his intimacy, not a substitute for it. He stopped striving for approval and started operating from acceptance.

The Lesson: Your competence will take you only as far as your character can sustain you. The hidden season is where you reinforce the foundation. If you skip this step, the height of your building will eventually expose the weakness of your basement.

Action Step: Schedule a "Audit of the Soul." Take one day away. Ask yourself: *If I gained the world tomorrow, what part of my character would crack under the weight? Is it my pride, my insecurity, my lust, or my anger?* Start fixing that crack now, while the lights are off.

Emotional Reinvention (The Single Parent's Crucible)

We often think of Joseph as a corporate figure, but he was also a man deeply estranged from family. He was alone. He was single. He was isolated. He had no support system.

Let's look at **The Single Parent** as a modern archetype of this struggle.

Consider **Maria**.

Maria is a single mother of two. Her husband left, leaving a wake of debt and emotional debris. Her finances are tight. She feels the walls of the "prison" closing in. The "Victim" script tells her she is abandoned, overwhelmed, and statistically destined to fail. Society tells her she is broken.

The "Joseph" script tells her she is in training. She is the head of a future dynasty. She realizes that her children are watching how she handles the "pit." She understands that her response to this crisis will form the emotional blueprint for her children's lives.

Maria chooses reinvention through self-efficacy—the belief in her capacity to execute behaviors necessary to produce specific performance attainments. She refuses to be a statistic.

She begins by investing in therapy and healing. Even with limited funds, she prioritizes counseling to break the generational trauma, determined not to pass the bitterness to her "Ephraim and Manasseh." She knows that a healed mother is the most significant inheritance she can give, and she refuses to let her ex-husband rent space in her head for free.

Next, she commits to physical discipline, waking up early to exercise. As Tony Robbins says, "Physiology determines psychology." She knows she cannot be emotionally intense if she is physically lethargic. By changing her physical state, she interrupts the cortisol-stress loop, releasing endorphins and dopamine to carry the emotional load. She trains her body to tell her mind that she is strong.

Finally, she takes control of her financial planning. She stops looking for a rescue and starts looking for a budget. She educates herself on financial literacy, turning her scarcity into strategic stewardship. She learns to multiply the little she has.

She is not just raising kids; she is raising a dynasty. She is investing in the emotional equity of her future.

Reflective Invitation: *Are you waiting for a rescue, or are you building a raft? Joseph didn't wait for his brothers to rescue him. He bloomed where he was planted until God moved him. What does "building a raft" look like in your life today?*

Personal Branding in the Dark

John Maxwell teaches the Law of the Picture: "People do what people see." Leadership is visual. It is modeled, not just taught.

What did the cupbearer and the baker see in Joseph? Genesis 40:6 says, *"When Joseph came to them in the morning, he saw that they were troubled."*

Wait. Joseph is in prison. He is the victim. He is the one who should be troubled. He is the one who should be demanding comfort. Yet, he is the one noticing the countenance of others. **This is the brand.** This is high-level **Emotional Intelligence (EQ)**. Even in the depths of his own suffering, Joseph retained the capacity for empathy. He did not allow his pain to make him narcissistic or self-absorbed. He kept his eyes outward.

Personal Branding in the Kingdom is not about a logo, a website, a curated Instagram feed, or a viral LinkedIn post. It is about the consistency of character. It is about who you are when the accolades are gone.

Joseph's brand was a triad of excellence, integrity, and prophetic insight. He served Potiphar, the Jailer, and the prisoners with the same level of commitment. He didn't adjust his effort based on the prestige of his audience, nor did he save his "best self" for Pharaoh. When the moment came two years later and Pharaoh needed an answer, the cupbearer didn't say, "I know a guy who wants a job." He said, "I know a man who has the Spirit of the Gods in him." He remembered Joseph's brand because Joseph lived it in the dark.

You build your reputation when no one is watching. The palace's lights reveal only what was built in the dark of the prison. If you cheat in the dark, you will fail in the light. If you are lazy in obscurity, you will be incompetent in opportunity.

Action Step: Define your "Hidden Brand." If the people currently in your "prison" (your difficult boss, your annoying coworkers, your estranged family members) were asked to describe you, what three words would they use? If those words aren't "faithful, wise, discerning," change your behavior today.

The Palace Reveal

"Then Pharaoh sent and called Joseph, and they quickly brought him out of the pit. And when he had shaved himself and changed his clothes, he came in before Pharaoh." — Genesis 41:14

It happened quickly. Thirteen years of slowness, then one hour of sudden acceleration. This is the nature of the Kingdom: long preparation, sudden promotion. God often moves slowly, then suddenly. But look closely at the archeology of the moment.

When the call came, Joseph didn't just walk in looking like a Hebrew slave. He understood **Cultural Intelligence (CQ)**. The text says explicitly that he *"shaved himself."* To a Hebrew, the beard was a sign of dignity, maturity, and masculinity. To cut it was often a sign of shame. To the Ancient Egyptians, however, facial hair was often considered unclean or a sign of mourning/low status. The Egyptian elite were meticulously clean-shaven, often shaving their entire bodies to maintain purity and hygiene.

Joseph invested in the Protocol of the Palace before he had the Position. He shed his cultural preference to gain strategic influence. He realized that to reach the king, *he had to remove the* *barrier of prejudice.* He didn't compromise his God (he gave God all the glory in his speech), but he adapted his method. He was "all things to all men" long before Paul wrote the epistle. He understood that his message was too important to be rejected because of his appearance.

The subsequent investiture confirms this transformation. When Pharaoh promotes him, he gifts him a signet ring, fine linen, and a gold chain (Genesis 41:42). These aren't random gifts; they are the specific insignias of the **Vizier** (*Tjaty*), the highest official in the land next to Pharaoh. The **signet ring** gave him the Power of Attorney; his stamp was as good as Pharaoh's signature, allowing him to execute laws and move treasuries. The **fine linen** marked his membership in the priestly and noble class, separating him from the commoners and symbolizing purity. The **gold chain**—identified by archeologists as the "Gold of Valor" (*nebu n qen*)—was an Egyptian honor usually reserved for military heroes who returned from battle victorious. Joseph was decorated as a warrior, not for fighting an army, but for fighting a coming economic collapse. He was recognized as a savior of the state.

Because he had invested strategically during the drought, he was ready to manage the abundance. He didn't need on-the-job training; he had already graduated.

The Executive Strategy (Managing the Famine)

We often marvel at Joseph's interpretation of the dream, but interpretation is not management. Pharaoh didn't promote Joseph just because he was a mystic or a dreamer; he promoted him because he was a strategic planner. Joseph presented a comprehensive fourteen-year macro-economic forecast and a crisis management plan. This is where "spiritual formation" meets "business administration."

Joseph's strategy rested on four pillars. First was **Strategic Foresight**. He recognized that the economy is cyclical, predicting a "Bull Market" of seven plenteous years followed by a catastrophic "Bear Market" of seven years of famine. While most leaders are myopic, consuming everything during the surplus, strategic leaders conserve during the boom to survive the bust.

Second, he implemented the **20% Protocol**. He implemented a national savings rate, taking one-fifth of the land's produce during the years of plenty. In modern management terms, this is Counter-Cyclical Investment. While the population was consuming 100% of their yield, Joseph enforced a 20% liquidity reserve. He didn't starve the people to save; he simply curbed the excess. He imposed discipline when motivation was low, effectively creating a Sovereign Wealth Fund of grain.

Third, he utilized **Supply Chain Resilience** through decentralization. Genesis 41:48 notes that he "put the food in the cities." Joseph did not haul all the grain to a central capital like Memphis or Thebes, which would have created a logistical nightmare involving massive transportation costs and theft risk. Instead, he utilized a decentralized distribution model, storing grain in the very cities where it was harvested. This reduced friction, mitigated risk by avoiding a single point of failure, and ensured that when the crisis hit, the solution was local.

Finally, he engaged in **Asset Consolidation**. During the famine, Joseph managed the transition from a barter economy to a centralized state economy (Genesis 47). He traded grain for money, then livestock, then land. While controversial to modern sensibilities, in the context of Ancient Near Eastern survival, this was Total Crisis Management. He prevented national collapse and anarchy by leveraging the state's assets to preserve the population, ensuring the state remained solvent so it could continue to feed the people.

The Lesson: You cannot pray your way out of a problem you behaved your way into. Joseph prayed, but he also planned. He combined faith with operational excellence.

Action Step: Look at your current "Season of Plenty" (where you have time, money, or energy). Are you consuming 100% of it? Institute a **"Joseph Tax"** on yourself. Save 20% of your income, your energy, or your time for the "lean years" that may come. Build your silo now.

My Reflection

My friends, fellow leaders, listen to me closely. Do not despise the day of small beginnings. Do not curse the prison walls. Do not resent the silence of the phone or the emptiness of the calendar.

We are living in a time that requires **Josephs**. The world is heading toward economic, emotional, and spiritual famines. The systems of this world are fragile. When they shake, the world will not look to the influencers, the celebrities, or the people who have only known the palace. They will look for leaders who have scars. They will look for leaders who have graduated from the University of the Pit.

They will need men and women who know how to interpret the times, who have the character to handle power without being corrupted by it, and who have the strategic mind to save a generation. They need leaders who have been hollowed out by God so they can be filled with His wisdom.

Your action plan for this season is clear. **Identify your Void** by naming the area of your life that feels empty or hidden, and stop running from it. **Sow the Seed** by determining what book you need to read, what habit you need to break, or what prayer you need to pray. Finally, **Serve the Prisoner**. Find someone in your current "mess" and serve them. Lift their head, even while yours is bowing low. That is the key to your promotion.

You are not forgotten. You are being forged. The heat is not to burn you; it is to purify the gold. Stop waiting. Start investing. **The Palace is coming. Be ready.**

If you are navigating a high-stakes transition and want to apply this framework to your own situation with clarity and discipline, scan the QR code below for a Transition Readiness Chat.

CHAPTER 8

THE WAITING ROOM PLAYBOOK: INFLUENCE, TRUST, AND NETWORKS IN THE HIDDEN SEASON

"Constraints are not limitations; they are design parameters."

— CHARLES EAMES

The Making of Confinement

If you examine the biography of almost any transformative leader, biblical hero, or historical giant, you will inevitably discover a gaping, unexplained hole in the timeline. It is a season that, on the surface, appears to be a burial—a period of lost time, wasted potential, and enforced silence.

It is the "wilderness years" of Moses tending sheep in the backside of the desert in Midian, far from the halls of power he was raised in, his Egyptian eloquence slowly buried under the dust of shepherding. It is the twenty-seven years in the prison cell of Nelson Mandela on Robben Island, breaking rocks in the blinding sun, transforming from a radical revolutionary into a statesman of reconciliation. It is the cave of Adullam where David hid from the madness of Saul, surrounded by a ragtag group of debtors, the distressed, and the discontented, learning to lead an army of misfits before he ever led a nation. However, upon closer, Spirit-led inspection, this season reveals itself not as a tomb, but as a womb;

not a burial, but a planting. We call this liminal space **The Waiting Room**.

For Joseph, the Waiting Room wasn't a sterile doctor's office with outdated magazines, soft jazz, and the promise of a scheduled appointment. It was a visceral, sensory nightmare. It was an Egyptian dungeon—specifically, a *beit sohar*. Linguists and archaeologists suggest the etymology implies a fortress structure, likely a "turret" or a silo-like fortification used for high-security prisoners.

Joseph wasn't merely thrown into a hole; he was inserted into the dark heart of the Egyptian military-industrial complex. He was surrounded by the noise of administration, the grinding of grain, and the machinery of the state. He was isolated from his family and his heritage, yet paradoxically, he was physically positioned closer to the seat of geopolitical power than he had ever been in the open fields of Canaan. He was in the basement of the ancient world's White House, learning the empire's rhythms from the bottom up. He was seeing the underside of the tapestry of Egyptian power, seeing the knots and the loose threads that the public never saw.

The Trauma of Erasure and Social Death: Psychologically, what Joseph faced is a phenomenon sociologist **Orlando Patterson** defines as *Social Death*. This is a condition often observed in chattel slavery, maximum-security incarceration, and extreme exile. When a human being is stripped of status, name, agency, and future prospects, the brain's defense mechanisms often trigger a severe "freeze" response.

The identity is assaulted on every level. Joseph was no longer "the beloved son" who wore the coat of many colors, a garment that signified favor and future authority. He was no longer "the overseer of Potiphar's house" who managed vast wealth and commanded servants. He was a number. He was a non-entity. He was erased from the civic register. In the ancient world, to be cut off from one's kin and land was equivalent to ceasing to exist. He had no legal standing, no advocate, and seemingly no future.

After repeated exposure to uncontrollable stressors (like electric shocks in dogs, or arbitrary cruelty in humans), an individual feels that no amount of effort will change the outcome, so they cease all attempts at constructive action. They stop planning. They stop grooming. They stop hoping. The brain literally rewires itself to accept defeat as the baseline reality. The victim becomes passive, believing that any action is futile.

In this state, **Abraham Maslow's Hierarchy of Needs** collapses completely. When safety and physiological needs are threatened daily—when you don't know if you will be fed, beaten, or executed—the higher-level needs of esteem, belonging, and self-actualization typically vanish. Survival becomes the only objective. Most people, when they hit this level of the Waiting Room, disassociate or disintegrate. They internalize the external chaos, allowing the prison around them to become a prison within them. They become bitter, cynical, or broken.

In this chapter, we are going to dismantle the pervasive myth that you must wait for a title, a promotion, or a corner office to be a leader. We are going to explore how Joseph built a massive network of influence—social capital—in the most unlikely, resource-poor place on earth.

Leading When You Lack Authority

John C. Maxwell famously teaches the **Law of the Lid**: *Leadership ability is the lid that determines a person's level of effectiveness.* If a person's leadership ability is a four on a scale of one to ten, their effectiveness will never rise above a three. The organization is always limited by the leader. You cannot outsource leadership; the constraint is always at the top. If the leader is a lid, the organization cannot grow.

When Joseph entered the prison, the "lid" was physically clamped down tight. He had zero positional authority. He was a convict. A foreigner. A slave. In the rigid, stratified corporate hierarchy of Ancient Egypt, a society obsessed with order (*Ma'at*) and hierarchy, he was a negative integer. He had no budget, no staff, no timeline for release, and no legal rights. He was at the absolute bottom of the social pyramid.

But leadership is not a title; leadership is influence. Nothing more, nothing less. It is the ability to mobilize others toward a common goal, regardless of your rank on the org chart. It is the capacity to create movement where there is stagnation, to create order where there is chaos.

How does a convict become the warden's CEO? How does a prisoner become the de facto ruler of his own cage?

The Shadow Organization and Operational Excellence

Joseph didn't start with a charismatic vision speech; he started with operational excellence. In modern management theory, this is the non-negotiable foundation of trust. Before you can lead change, you must demonstrate competence. You must show that you can handle the "small things" with absolute precision. You must prove that you are a steward of the present before you can be entrusted with the future.

Joseph essentially implemented a system of management by exception. This is a style of business management that focuses on identifying and handling cases that deviate from the norm. Imagine the daily logistics of a political prison in the Bronze Age. It wasn't just locking doors; it was running a small city.

First, consider the logistical nightmare of resource allocation. Joseph had to distribute scarce food rations equitably to prevent riots. In a famine-prone region, food security starts in the micro-ecosystems. Joseph likely developed a system that minimized theft and ensured transparent distribution, preventing the weak from being exploited by the strong.

Second, he mastered conflict resolution. He was tasked with mediating disputes between high-stress, potentially violent inmates. A prison is a powder keg of repressed rage and fear. Joseph became the coolant. He de-escalated conflicts before they required the guards' intervention, likely using the wisdom and diplomacy that would later serve him in Pharaoh's court.

Third, he oversaw sanitation and health, managing waste and sickness in a confined space to prevent plague. In an underground cistern, disease is a death sentence. Joseph likely enforced strict hygiene protocols, anticipating the Levitical laws he would later see his people adopt, understanding that cleanliness was crucial for survival.

Finally, he handled inventory tracking, ensuring the guards' supplies and the prisoners' quotas were accounted for. He likely managed the ledger, tracking every loaf of bread and every jar of water, creating a system of accountability that the Warden had never seen before.

Joseph mastered these systems. He created such a reliable ecosystem of delegation, logistics, and oversight that the Warden "paid no attention to anything that was in Joseph's charge" (Gen 39:23).

The Warden effectively outsourced his entire job to Joseph because Joseph removed the friction from the Warden's life. The Warden only had to get involved if there was an exception—a riot, a death, or a high-level transfer. Everything else was Joseph.

This created what organizational theorists call a shadow organization. While the org chart on the wall said the Warden was in charge, the *actual* flow of information, decisions, and power went through Joseph. He was the informal node that connected every part of the system. He held the "institutional memory" and the operational keys. He was the indispensable man.

The lesson here is simple but profound: **Autonomy is earned through reliability.** If your boss has to micromanage you, your influence is shrinking. If your boss can ignore you because your results are guaranteed, your influence is expanding. Joseph bought his freedom of movement inside the prison with the currency of competence. He proved that even in chains, he was free to excel.

In addition, Joseph mastered what Tony Robbins calls **State Management**. Most people in prison exist in a low-energy state of suffering, focused on what they've lost, focused on the injustice, focused on the pain. When you are in a state of suffering, you are resource-poor. You cannot see opportunities; you can only see obstacles. You are biologically incapable of strategic thought because your brain is in survival mode.

Joseph consciously shifted his state. He moved from "Why is this happening to me?" to "What is needed in this room?" By shifting his focus from his *problem* to his *purpose*, he unlocked his own resourcefulness. He hacked his own biology to remain a leader in a place designed to make him a slave. He chose to act rather than be acted upon.

In your current "Waiting Room," whether that's a mid-level management role where you feel invisible, a career plateau, or a season of unemployment—are you waiting for authority to lead, or are you creating influence by solving problems for those above you?

The Power Behind the Title

We must be careful not to read modern definitions into ancient titles. These weren't kitchen staff or lowly servants. In the complex bureaucracy of the Middle Kingdom administration, the "chief cupbearer" and "chief baker" were cabinet-level officials. They were aristocrats who wielded immense power.

The **cupbearer** wasn't just pouring wine; he was the final security checkpoint for the king's life. He tasted for poison. He stood at the right hand of the Pharaoh during feasts and councils. He had the Pharaoh's ear during his most relaxed moments. He was a confidant, a gatekeeper, and a man of immense political sway. He controlled access to the throne, determining who got to speak to the god-king.

The **baker** was equally powerful. He controlled the royal food supply and the vast granaries that fed the palace. In an era where poisoning was the primary method of assassination, these men were the Secret Service of their day. They managed vast staffs and logistics networks, overseeing the nutritional security of the royal court.

Their imprisonment suggests a major security breach or a foiled assassination plot against the Pharaoh. They were likely being held while an investigation was conducted to see who was the conspirator and who was innocent. When Joseph served them, he wasn't just serving common inmates; he was networking with the disgraced elite of the Egyptian government. He was gaining access to the C-Suite of Egypt, right there in the dungeon.

Situational Leadership and MBWA

Ken Blanchard's model of **Servant Leadership** turns the traditional pyramid upside down. The leader exists to serve the people, not the other way around. In a typical prison hierarchy, the "trustee" or head prisoner uses their power to exploit others for better food, protection, or favors. It is a predatory hierarchy where the strong eat the weak. Joseph reversed this. Despite being the functional manager of the prison, he adopted the posture of a servant. He did not use his position to exploit these wealthy prisoners; he used it to minister to them.

He also practiced what Tom Peters (in *In Search of Excellence*) calls **Management by Wandering Around (MBWA)**. He didn't just sit in the administrative office delegating tasks; he walked the floor. He kept his finger on the pulse of the organization. He was present. He knew the mood of the cellblock.

Emotional Intelligence and the Ministry of Noticing

Don't miss the profound **Emotional Intelligence (EQ)** in that verse. Joseph has his own massive problems. He is the victim of a miscarriage of justice. He is living in a traumatic environment. But he notices the countenance of others. He steps outside of his own pain to acknowledge the pain of another.

Neuroscience tells us about **Mirror Neurons**, brain cells that react both when we perform an action and when we observe someone else performing it. They are the biological basis of empathy. In high-stress, survival-based environments (like a prison, a combat zone, or a toxic corporate culture), people usually shut down their mirror neurons to protect themselves. This is called "compassion fatigue" or "empathic distress." To survive, we put up emotional walls. We stop seeing people as *people* and start seeing them as *threats* or competitors for resources.

Joseph fought against this biological urge to isolate. He kept his mirror neurons firing. He stayed open. He noticed the micro-expressions of anxiety and fear on the faces of the cupbearer and Baker. He read the room, and then he acted.

First, **he initiated**. He didn't wait for them to ask for help. He broke the silence. He stepped into the awkwardness. He risked rejection to offer connection.

Next, **he inquired**. He asked open-ended questions about their emotional state. He validated their feelings. He didn't offer a platitude; he offered a listening ear.

Finally, **he interpreted**. He brought God's wisdom into their confusion. He connected their earthly reality with spiritual truth.

This interaction also highlights the concept of **Psychological Safety** (coined by Amy Edmondson). In a prison environment defined by fear and silence, Joseph created a "safe container" where these men felt comfortable sharing their vulnerabilities—specifically, their disturbing dreams. They trusted him with their subconscious fears because he had established a baseline of care in their conscious reality. They knew he was for them, not against them.

Reflective Invitation: When you walk into your office, your job site, or your home, do you see faces? Or do you just see functions? Do you see "the accountant" or do you see "Sakura, who looks tired"? Do you see the "waitress" or do you see a person carrying a heavy tray and a heavier heart? *Social capital is earned when you care about people before you need them.*

Unlikely Alliances and The Prophetic Network

Developing Relationships with "Connectors"

The Cupbearer and the baker represent two types of relationships we encounter in the Waiting Room.

First is the **Dead End**, represented by the baker. Some relationships are for a season, and they end in loss. Joseph ministered to the baker with truth, even though the news was horrific (execution). A leader must have the courage to deliver hard truths, what Kim Scott calls **Radical Candor**—caring personally while challenging directly. Joseph did not give the baker false hope just to be liked; he gave him the truth to prepare him for the end. This shows high integrity. Leadership is not always about delivering good news; it is about delivering *true* news. It is about having the backbone to say what needs to be said, even when it is painful.

Second is the **Conduit**, represented by the cupbearer. This was the strategic alliance. The Cupbearer was Joseph's bridge to the palace.

The Strength of Weak Ties

Mark Granovetter's famous sociological theory, **The Strength of Weak Ties**, posits that job opportunities and breakthroughs rarely come from your close friends (strong ties) because they know the same people you know. Your strong ties are in your same social bubble. Breakthroughs come from "weak ties"—acquaintances who bridge you to a *different* social cluster.

The cupbearer was a weak tie. He belonged to a world Joseph had zero access to: the royal court. He spoke a different corporate language. He knew the protocols of the throne room. By serving this weak tie, Joseph planted a seed in a completely different ecosystem. He invested in a relationship that seemed dormant but held the code to his future. He served a man who could not help him in the moment, believing that the relationship had value beyond the transaction.

The Dream Culture

Joseph's willingness to interpret dreams was a high-stakes move. The Egyptians were obsessed with dreams. The *Chester Beatty Papyrus III* (The Egyptian Dream Book) shows us that Egyptians believed dreams were a zone of contact between the living and the divine. By stepping into the role of interpreter, Joseph was stepping into a priestly, almost magical function. He was asserting spiritual authority over Egyptian cosmology. He was positioning himself not just as an administrator, but as a seer—a man who had the "Spirit of the Holy Gods" in him. He was claiming a connection to the divine that superseded the Egyptian pantheon.

He gave the cupbearer massive value. And then, he made a request. *"But remember me when it is well with you, and please show me kindness and mention me to Pharaoh, and get me out of this house."* (Genesis 40:14).

However, the story takes a brutal, heart-wrenching turn. *"Yet the chief cupbearer did not remember Joseph, but forgot him."* (Genesis 40:23).

Tony Robbins' Principle of Massive Action vs. Patience

We are taught to take massive action. Joseph took action. He interpreted the dream. He made the ask. He did everything right. And... nothing happened. What do you do when your massive action yields zero results? You have to master the **Art of Active Waiting**. Active waiting is not passive resignation. It is continuing to sharpen your skills, build your character, and serve your community while the external circumstances remain unchanged. It is tilling the soil when there is no rain. It is preparing the vessel even when there is no oil.

If Joseph had become bitter during those two years, he would have rotted. If he had let resentment calcify his heart toward the cupbearer, he would not have been ready when the call finally came. He had to keep running the prison. He had to keep serving. He had to keep his faith in a God who seemed silent. He had to trust that the delay was not a denial, but a preparation.

The Leadership Lab

Practical Applications for the Modern Professional

How do we apply the "Dungeon Strategy" to our corporate careers, our ministries, and our businesses? Here are three laws of "Waiting Room Relationships" to practice this week.

1. The Law of the Second Mile

In a transactional world, be transformational. Everyone does the bare minimum to keep their job. This is the "quiet quitting" phenomenon. In the prison, Joseph went the second mile. He didn't just guard the prisoners; he cared for them. He provided emotional labor when only physical labor was required.

Imagine you are a project manager. You have a vendor who is late on a deliverable. The transactional response is to send a demanding email citing the contract and penalties. The "Second Mile" response is to call them and say, "I know you guys are swamped, and I see the pressure you are under. Is there a blocker on your end that I can help remove to get this across the line? How can I help you win?" The result is that you transform a vendor into a partner. You build social capital that pays dividends in the next crisis. You move from a contract-based relationship to a trust-based relationship.

Action: Identify one person in your professional circle who can do *nothing* for you right now—an intern, a receptionist, a struggling peer, a junior developer. Invest fifteen minutes this week in adding value to them. Listen to their story. Offer a resource. Mentorship is not about cloning yourself; it's about serving others.

2. The Law of Emotional Mechanics

You cannot influence others if you cannot control your own state. If you walk into work depressed, anxious, or bitter about your lack of promotion, you repel social capital. Emotions are contagious. If you are the source of anxiety, people will avoid you. If you are the source of certainty and calm, people will flock to you.

Consider a scenario where your company just announced a restructuring. Rumors are flying, and panic is setting in. You are worried about your own job. The **Low State** response is to gossip by the coffee machine, amplifying the fear, checking the news obsessively, and slumping in your chair. You become an energy vampire. The **Peak State** response is to take a walk, breathe, pray, and reset. You ask yourself, "What is the opportunity here?" You walk into the team meeting with your shoulders back and say, "Okay, everyone, there is a lot of noise, but let's focus on what we can control today. Let's execute on the mission." You become an anchor in the storm.

Action: Change your physiology. Before you walk into a high-stakes meeting, reset your focus. Ask yourself: *Who needs certainty in this room? How can I be the thermostat that sets the temperature, rather than the thermometer that just reflects it?*

3. The Law of the Inner Circle

Joseph's network was small, but it was potent. He didn't try to know everyone. He focused on the people God placed immediately in front of him. He didn't try to network with Pharaoh from the dungeon; that was impossible. He networked with the cupbearer. He stewarded the relationships he had access to.

If you want to be the VP of marketing, but you are ignoring your current director because you think they are incompetent or unimportant, you are making a critical error. The fix is to bloom where you are planted. Serve your direct supervisor with such excellence that they cannot help but praise you to the upper management. Your "cupbearer" might be your current boss, or a colleague in a different department who is about to be promoted. Stop looking "over" people to get to the "important" people. The person next to you holds the keys.

Action: Stop trying to network with the CEO if you haven't served your direct supervisor. Serve the "cupbearers" in your life—the people who are passing through your department on their way to somewhere else. Serve them so well that even if they forget you for two years, when the crisis comes, your name is the first on their lips.

Your Prison is Your Platform

Brothers and sisters, I don't know what "prison" you are in today. I don't know if you are in a cubicle that feels like a coffin, a marriage that feels like a sentence, or a financial hole that feels like a dungeon. I don't know if you have been falsely accused, overlooked, or forgotten.

But I know this: **God wastes nothing.**

The Waiting Room is not a holding pattern; it is a forging fire. The relationships you are navigating right now (the difficult boss, the forgetful colleague, the needy client) these are not distractions from your destiny. They *are* the path to your destiny.

Joseph was seventeen when he was sold into slavery. He was 30 when he stood before Pharaoh. That is thirteen years. Thirteen years of waiting. Thirteen years of serving when no one was watching. Thirteen years of building character, resilience, and faith. Thirteen years of learning Egyptian administration, economics, and leadership from the bottom up.

Do not despise the day of small beginnings. Do not despise the dungeon. It is in the dark that the root system grows deep enough to support the weight of the fruit that is coming.

Look around you today. Who needs their dream interpreted? Who needs a touch of kindness? Who needs a leader to rise up, despite the chains, and say, "God is in this place"?

Lift your head. Shave your face. Change your countenance. The King is about to call your name. But until he does ... **Serve the prisoner next to you.**

That is how you turn a waiting room into a launchpad.

If you are navigating a high-stakes transition and want to apply this framework to your own situation with clarity and discipline, scan the QR code below for a Transition Readiness Chat.

CHAPTER 9

Readiness Before Recognition: The Hidden Work Behind Visible Success

"Success is the sum of small efforts, repeated day in and day out."

— Robert Collier

Introduction: The Illusion of the "Suddenly"

We live in a hyper-accelerated culture that is obsessively fixated on the myth of the "overnight success." We scroll through LinkedIn feeds and industry headlines, assaulted by images of the meteoric rise: the thirty-under-thirty promotion that defies seniority, the tech IPO that mints billionaires in a morning, the viral hit that launches a career, or the massive ministry expansion that seems to happen by divine fiat. We perceive these moments as singular, isolated events—lightning strikes of fortune that descend upon the lucky few. We become voyeurs of victory, addicted to the highlight reels of others while despairing over our own behind-the-scenes footage.

This perception is the "Iceberg Illusion." We see the 10% that glimmers above the water (the public accolades, the title, the wealth, the applause) but we remain willfully blind to the ninety percent of mass hidden beneath the surface. We ignore the crushing atmospheric pressure that built for years to create the storm. We ignore the cold, dark, lonely years of character formation that support the weight of the visible success. We fail to see the failed prototypes, the lonely nights of study, the silent prayers that seemed to hit the ceiling, and the grinding discipline required to forge a character capable of sustaining the weight of glory. We want the "suddenly" of Pentecost without the tarrying of the Upper Room. We want the resurrection power without the crucifixion process.

Psychologically, our brains are wired to pay attention to contrast—the sudden change from zero to hero. The human mind seeks the dopamine hit of the "before and after" picture, ignoring the grueling, monotonous middle. We crave the transformation montage in the movie, skipping the three years of actual training it represents. We ignore the plateau of latent potential where growth is happening but evidence is invisible. We live in a microwave generation that demands crockpot results, forgetting that what is heated quickly cools quickly, but what is cooked slowly retains its heat.

If you are reading this, chances are you feel a painful gap between your potential and your reality. You feel a stirring in your spirit—a "God-sized" dream that feels undeniable—yet your Monday morning reality feels mundane, perhaps even invisible. You are doing the work, but nobody is watching. You are grinding in the dark, wondering if the light will ever break through. You may be asking, "If God called me, why am I hidden? If I have this potential, why am I in this pit?"

Let me tell you something that might shift your entire psychology: **Obscurity is not a punishment; it is a prerequisite.**

In the economy of the Kingdom, and indeed in the immutable laws of leadership, private victories always precede public accolades. God is not hiding you because He is angry with you; He is hiding you *for* a purpose. He is incubating you. You are in the "darkroom" of development, where the image of who you are becoming is being etched onto your soul. Just as photographic film must be developed in total darkness to avoid being ruined by premature exposure to light, your character must be formed in the shadows before it can withstand the spotlight of success. Exposure without development leads to exposure of nakedness; development without exposure leads to readiness.

In this chapter, we are going to deconstruct the "Law of Process." We are going to look at the life of Joseph—not just as a Sunday School story, but as a masterclass in executive readiness, emotional intelligence, and spiritual maturity. We will witness the collision of thirteen years of grueling preparation with one singular moment of opportunity before the most powerful man on earth.

We will examine how a junior analyst mastering Excel spreadsheets is no different than Joseph managing the prison roster. We will see how a songwriter in a basement is mirroring the spiritual discipline of waiting. And we will prove that when the palace calls, and it will call, you won't have time to get ready. You must *be* ready.

Prepare your mind. Adjust your posture. It is time to master the art of the defining moment.

The University of Obscurity

The Pit and the Prison as Training Grounds

John C. Maxwell often speaks of the "Law of the Lid"—the idea that your leadership ability determines your level of effectiveness. If your leadership is a four, your effectiveness can never be higher than a three. For Joseph, the favorite son of Jacob, his "lid" was his ego and his immaturity. At seventeen, he had the vision (the dreams of sheaves and stars), but he lacked the character to carry the cargo. He had the gifting, but he lacked the grounding. He possessed the prophetic insight to see the future, but not the political wisdom to navigate the present. He knew *what* God was going to do, but he had no idea *how* to become the man who could do it.

God, in His severe mercy, enrolled Joseph in the "University of Obscurity." This wasn't a punishment for his dreams, but a preparation for his destiny. The curriculum consisted of three brutal courses, each designed to strip away a layer of the false self: The Pit, Potiphar's House, and the Prison.

1. The Pit: The Death of Entitlement

When Joseph was thrown into the cistern (Genesis 37), it was a violent stripping away of identity. The "coat of many colors"—his badge of distinction, his father's favor, and his social status—was torn from him. He was left naked and vulnerable in the dark. The silence of the pit was the first time Joseph had to listen to something other than his father's praise. It was the death of his entitlement. It was the moment he realized that the world owed him nothing, and that his dream would not be handed to him on a silver platter, but fought for on a battlefield of betrayal.

The Price of a Life: The biblical text notes a chilling detail: Joseph was sold for "twenty shekels of silver" (Genesis 37:28). Skeptics often dismiss Genesis as a much later invention, but this specific price tag serves as an archaeological fingerprint that validates the text's historicity. Records from the Code of Hammurabi and documents from Mari (18th century B.C.) confirm that the average price of a slave in the early second millennium was exactly twenty shekels.

By the time of Moses (c. 1400 B.C.), the price had risen to thirty shekels (Exodus 21:32). By the Assyrian period (c. 700 B.C.), inflation had driven the price to over fifty shekels. The text preserves the accurate economic data of Joseph's specific era.

This detail is vital for us today because it reminds us that your struggle is real, it is historical, and it has a "market price." Joseph was commoditized. To the world, he was worth exactly twenty pieces of silver. He was a line item on a trader's ledger, valued at the cost of a few months' labor or a handful of livestock. He had to learn that his value did not come from the market, but from his Maker. You are not suffering in a vacuum; you are part of a timeline of faithful men and women who have been undervalued by the world while being highly valued by heaven. When the world puts a price tag on you that is far below your worth, you must rely on the currency of heaven to maintain your solvency.

Breaking Identity Foreclosure: Developmental psychologists talk about "Identity Foreclosure"—a state where a young person locks into an identity (e.g., "the favorite son," "the smart one," "the athlete") without exploring or suffering. This creates a fragile ego because the identity is based on external validation rather than internal solidity. If you take away the "favorite son's" coat, who is he? If you take away the athlete's jersey, is he still valuable?

The Pit forced Joseph out of foreclosure. It was a trauma that shattered his assumed identity. By stripping away external validation, God forced Joseph to build a self-concept that wasn't dependent on his father's praise or his brothers' submission. He had to find out who he was in the dark, when he was worth only twenty shekels. He had to learn to be a son of God before he could be a ruler of men. He had to move from an identity received from his father to an identity forged with his Father.

2. Potiphar's House: Stewardship in Servitude

Sold into slavery in Egypt, Joseph enters the household of Potiphar, the captain of the guard. This is a critical pivot point. Most people in this situation would succumb to the "victim mentality" or "learned helplessness." A victim asks, "Why me? I am a son of Jacob! I shouldn't be scrubbing floors! This is beneath me. I am destined for greatness, not grit." They wait for the circumstances to change before they change their attitude.

But a leader's mentality asks, "I am here. How can I serve? How can I add value? How can I dominate this domain?" Joseph realized that while he could not choose his circumstances, he could choose his standard of performance. He instituted what we might call "The Joseph Standard"—doing menial tasks with monarchial dignity. He treated the floor he scrubbed as if it were the throne he would one day sit upon.

Ken Blanchard teaches us that "Servant Leadership is love in action." It is the belief that leadership is not about being served, but about serving. Joseph didn't wait for a promotion to start leading. He led *up*. He organized. He managed assets. He mastered the language and culture of Egypt while still a slave. He treated Potiphar's household as if it were his own. The scriptures record that Potiphar eventually "did not concern himself with anything except the food he ate." This implies total trust and total delegation.

Managing Up: Joseph mastered the art of "managing up," effectively buying back his leader's mental bandwidth. In modern corporate environments, this is the transition from being a "task doer" to an "owner." The task doer waits for instructions, asks what to do, and returns with problems, requiring high maintenance and constant supervision. The owner, conversely, anticipates needs, observes the leader's pain points, and solves them before they are verbalized. They return with completed tasks and solutions, becoming an asset that appreciates in value.

Joseph became the chief of staff for a high-ranking Egyptian official. He learned supply chain management, household economics, and personnel oversight on a micro-scale. He was practicing for the palace in the practice field of the pantry. He learned that if you can be faithful with a master's inventory, you can eventually be trusted with a nation's economy.

Consider **Vince**, a junior data analyst at a sprawling fintech firm.

His job is monotonous: cleaning data sets, debugging SQL

queries, and generating reports that senior management barely glances at. He feels overqualified, underutilized, and invisible. He watches peers get promoted while he stays late fixing broken spreadsheets. The temptation to "quiet quit"—to do the absolute minimum required to not get fired—is overwhelming.

He stands at a crossroads with two distinct options. He can choose the path of the victim, doing the bare minimum and complaining at happy hour about "management" and "the system." In this scenario, he passively waits for a better offer or a recruiter to rescue him, viewing his current role as a prison sentence and performing at the level of his wage, not the level of his potential.

Alternatively, he can choose the path of Joseph, utilizing cognitive reframing and managing up. Vince can reframe the "boring work" as "deep practice." He decides to master Python on his own time to automate the cleaning process, reducing a four-hour task to fifteen minutes. He uses the extra time to dig deeper into the data, eventually noticing patterns in customer churn that the C-suite is missing. He builds a predictive model—not because anyone asked, but because he is practicing excellence in the dark. He treats the company's data as if it were his own business.

Six months later, the VP of Strategy enters a board meeting in a panic; they are losing market share and don't know why. Vince is called in to pull a simple report. Instead, he presents his predictive model. He was ready. The "board presentation" fell in his lap, but he didn't stumble. He stood. He had already done the work when no one was watching.

3. The Prison: Leading When It's Unfair

If Potiphar's house was undergraduate studies, the Prison was the PhD program. Joseph was falsely accused of rape by Potiphar's wife, punished for his integrity, and thrown into the king's dungeon. This is the ultimate test of state management. It is one thing to serve when you are enslaved; it is another to serve when you are innocent and condemned. It challenges the fundamental belief that "good things happen to good people." It is the moment when theology collides with reality.

The Hebrew word for the dungeon here is distinctive. It likely refers to the Egyptian *Khnry* (criminal fortress) or the "Great Prison" known from Thebes. These were not modern correctional facilities with libraries and gyms; they were often forced labor centers or dark, subterranean holding tanks known as "The Round House."

The conditions were horrific—cramped, dark, smelling of despair, human waste, and rot. The Middle Kingdom prison system was brutal, designed to break the spirit through sensory deprivation and hopelessness. Yet, the text tells us, *"So the warden put Joseph in charge of all those held in the prison, and he was made responsible for all that was done there"* (Genesis 39:22). Even in hell, Joseph rose to management. He turned a dungeon into a department. He created order out of chaos in the darkest place of his life.

Internal Locus of Control: In psychology, people with an *External Locus of Control* believe life happens *to* them. They believe their emotional state is dictated by their environment, leading to thoughts like, "I'm depressed because I'm in prison," or "I'm angry because my boss is a jerk." This leads to victimhood and paralysis, making them thermometers that merely reflect the temperature of the room.

People with an *Internal Locus of Control* believe they can influence their outcomes, even in bad environments. They divorce their internal state from their external circumstances, acting as thermostats that set the temperature of the room. Joseph displayed a supreme Internal Locus of Control. He couldn't control the bars, the guards, or the timeline. But he *could* control his behavior, his attitude, and his work ethic. He practiced **executive administration** in a high-stress, high-confinement environment. He counseled fellow prisoners, developing high Emotional Intelligence (EQ). He learned to read the countenances of the baker and cupbearer, a skill he would later need to read the countenance of Pharaoh.

You are never "waiting" for a leadership position. You are leading right now. Your attitude in the "prison"—that dead-end job, that difficult marriage, that financial struggle—is the resume you are writing for Heaven. If you cannot lead a cell block, you will never lead a nation. If you cannot steward a season of scarcity, you will not be trusted with a season of surplus.

The Silent Grind

Developing Skills in the Dark

There is a pervasive myth in Christian circles that "favor" means you don't have to work hard. We often spiritualize laziness, expecting God to open doors we are not competent to walk through. This is textually and theologically inaccurate. Favor opened the door for Joseph, but competence kept him in the room. Favor got him the audience with Pharaoh, but wisdom got him the job.

During those years in prison, estimated to be at least two or three years, perhaps more, Joseph wasn't just praying; he was observing. He was learning the political structure of Egypt through the political prisoners he guarded. He was listening to the gossip of the court from the cupbearer and the baker. He was learning to interpret dreams—a spiritual gift, yes, but also a skill he honed through practice.

The Neurology of Deliberate Practice: Anders Ericsson, the psychologist behind the famous "10,000 Hour Rule," distinguishes between *naive practice* (just doing something repeatedly) and *deliberate practice* (stretching yourself beyond your current abilities with intent).

Naive practice is guarding the prisoners and doing the bare minimum to pass the time. Deliberate practice is studying them. The prison was Joseph's laboratory. He was rewiring his brain, neuroplasticity in action, learning to manage difficult, depressed, and volatile people. He was learning to interpret complex data (dreams) and deliver hard news with empathy (telling the baker he would be executed). He was developing the neural pathways of a ruler while wearing the chains of a prisoner.

Contemporary Case Study: The Songwriter

Makayla has been writing worship songs for eight years. She lives in a small, drafty apartment in Nashville, waiting tables at a diner to pay rent. She wakes up every morning at 5:00 AM to write until 7:00 AM before her shift starts. She smells like maple syrup and coffee, but her mind is on melody. She records demos that get minimal streams. She submits to publishers who return only silence or generic rejection letters. She plays to empty rooms on Tuesday nights, where the bartender is the only audience.

This is the "Silent Grind." It is the season where the work exceeds the reward. It is the sowing season where the ground looks barren, and the sky looks like brass. It is the season where the only applause you hear is the beat of your own heart.

But Makayla isn't just writing; she is studying the architecture of sound. She is analyzing why certain choruses lift a congregation and why others fall flat. She is dissecting the theology of hymns. She is applying **"Agile" methodology** to her art—iterating quickly, failing fast, and refining her product. She is building a catalog of excellence that no one hears.

One Tuesday, a producer she met three years ago calls out of the blue. A major artist is in the studio, and they are stuck on a bridge for a song that is due tomorrow. The energy in the studio is dead; they need a spark. "Do you have anything?" the producer asks, desperate.

If Makayla had spent the last eight years just "dreaming" of being big, or complaining about how hard the industry is, she would have nothing to offer. She would be empty-handed. But because she has been faithful in obscurity, she opens her laptop. She navigates to a folder titled "Bridges in B-Flat." She has fifteen options ready to go. She sends them over. The artist loves one. It becomes the hook of the song. She didn't get "lucky." She was prepared. The call was the opportunity; the folder on her laptop was the preparation.

The Law of the Big Mo (Momentum)

John Maxwell teaches the "Law of the Big Mo." Momentum is a leader's best friend. When you have momentum, problems seem small, and the future seems bright. But how do you build momentum when you are stuck in a cell? How do you create forward motion when your geography is static?

You build **internal momentum**. You grow your character when your circumstances are shrinking. You expand your mind when your walls are closing in. You deepen your prayer life when your social life is nonexistent. You read, you study, you workout, you forgive. Internal momentum is the pressure that builds up inside a champagne bottle; the outside looks still, but the inside is explosive. While the world sees you standing still, your spirit is running sprints.

Action Step: The Skill Audit

Stop waiting for the title and conduct a rigorous audit of your skills right now. First, assess your Hard Skills: what technical abilities does your "Palace" (your dream future) require? Do you need to know P&L management, public speaking, AI integration, or crisis management? Learn them now in the dark. Take the course, read the book, and become the expert before you become the executive. Second, evaluate your soft skills: how is your conflict resolution? Can you handle criticism without collapsing? Can you read a room? Can you motivate a team with no budget? Can you work with people you don't like (like Potiphar's wife or the warden)? Finally, test your Spiritual Skills: can you hear God's voice when you are in pain? Can you maintain your integrity when no one is watching? Can you forgive those who forgot you (like the cupbearer)?

The Call to the Palace

Recognizing the Defining Moment

"Then Pharaoh sent and called Joseph, and they brought him hastily out of the dungeon..." (Genesis 41:14 KJV)

The call usually comes when you least expect it. Joseph woke up that morning a prisoner. He ate prison food. He did his prison duties. He had no idea that by sunset, he would be prime minister of the greatest empire on earth. It was just another Tuesday in the dungeon until it wasn't.

Notice the urgency in the text: *"brought him hastily."* The Hebrew implies a rushing, a running. When the *kairos* (appointed/divine) moment arrives, *chronos* (linear/sequential) time accelerates. Years of delay are suddenly swallowed up in minutes of destiny. The waiting is long, but the promotion is instant.

The Protocol of the Palace: Shave and Change

Here is a detail we often miss, yet it is crucial for anyone aspiring to influence secular systems. Genesis 41:14 continues: *"...and he shaved himself, and changed his raiment, and came in unto Pharaoh."*

The Clash of Cultures

This seemingly minor detail is historically profound. Joseph was a Hebrew, and Semitic men wore full beards as a sign of masculinity, dignity, and tribal identity. To cut the beard was often a sign of mourning, shame, or madness (see 2 Samuel 10:4). His beard was his link to his father, Jacob, and his heritage. It was his visible identity.

However, Ancient Egyptians were fastidious about cleanliness. Herodotus and Egyptian tomb paintings reveal that Egyptian priests and courtiers shaved their entire bodies—heads, faces, and bodies—to be "pure" before the gods and the king. To a pharaoh, a bearded man was unclean, a barbarian, a "sand-dweller," a shepherd (which was an "abomination" to Egyptians).

Joseph faced a critical choice in that split second: *Hold onto his cultural preference and personal comfort, or adapt to the protocol of the opportunity?* He could have insisted, "I am a Hebrew! Take me as I am! My beard is my truth! I won't conform to your pagan standards!" If he had done that, the beard would have become the focus. Pharaoh would have been distracted by the "uncleanliness" and likely missed the message. Instead, Joseph shaved. He didn't compromise his theology (he gives God all the glory in verse 16), but he adjusted his methodology. He removed the barrier that would have distracted Pharaoh. He understood that to influence the culture, he had to be intelligible to the culture. He engaged in "Missional Adaptation," becoming all things to all men that he might save some (or in this case, save the nation).

Executive Presence

In corporate strategy, this is known as **Executive Presence**. It is the "X-factor" that determines whether you are taken seriously in the boardroom. It comprises three pillars. First is Gravitas: how you act, and whether you project calm and confidence under pressure. Second is Communication: how you speak, and whether you are clear, concise, and compelling. Third is Appearance: how you look, and whether you look like you belong in the room.

Joseph understood that to be heard by the C-Suite (Pharaoh), he had to look like he belonged in the C-Suite. He removed the friction of cognitive dissonance. If he had walked in looking like a prisoner, Pharaoh would have underestimated the solution. He dressed for the destination, not the dungeon. He respected the protocol of the palace enough to adapt his presentation without altering his message.

Parker is a middle manager in logistics. He has been studying leadership theory at night, getting an MBA online while raising three kids. He is exhausted, overworked, and feels stuck. He feels like a cog in a machine that doesn't know his name.

Suddenly, the company announces a merger. Chaos ensues. The regional director quits in protest. Rumors fly. The stock price dips. The CEO calls an emergency town hall meeting. The atmosphere is toxic with fear.

Parker recognizes the moment. He "shaves and changes clothes"—metaphorically. While his colleagues are panicking, gossiping in the breakroom, or frantically updating their resumes, Parker shifts his demeanor from "employee" to "leader." He puts on a suit (or the industry equivalent of "ready"). He walks into the chaos with a calm, grounded presence. He sits in the front row. He has already prepared a one-page integration strategy, outlining the three biggest risks to the supply chain during the merger and proposing solutions. He has anticipated the questions no one else is asking.

When the CEO opens the floor and asks, "Does anyone have a handle on the western distribution centers?", the room is silent. Parker stands up. He doesn't just raise his hand; he speaks the language of the solution, not the problem. He hands the CEO his one-pager. He becomes the best candidate for the new regional director role not because of his tenure, but because of his readiness. He maximized the crisis. He stepped into the vacuum of leadership that fear created.

The Psychology of Presence: Overriding the Amygdala

When Joseph stood before Pharaoh, he wasn't trembling. He was respectful, but he was authoritative. Biologically, standing before a king who could execute you on a whim, a "living god" who held the power of life and death, should trigger an **Amygdala Hijack**. This is when the brain's primitive fear center detects a threat and floods the body with cortisol and adrenaline. It shuts down the prefrontal cortex (the center of logic, language, and strategy) and prepares the body for Fight, Flight, or Freeze. Most people would stutter, sweat, or collapse.

How did Joseph stay calm? How did he access the wisdom to interpret the dream and design a national strategy in that high-pressure moment? Because he had already faced the worst. He had faced death in the pit. He had faced the seduction and betrayal of Potiphar's wife. He had faced the crushing disappointment of being forgotten by the cupbearer. Repeated exposure to stressors, combined with deep faith, creates **stress inoculation**. Joseph had learned to regulate his nervous system in the dark. He knew that if God could sustain him in a pit, God could sustain him in a palace. He knew Pharaoh was powerful, but he knew Yahweh was supreme. As Tony Robbins teaches, your state dictates your story. If you are in a state of fear, you will tell a story of weakness. If you are in a state of faith, you will tell a story of power. Joseph entered that throne room in a "Peak State" of certainty—not in himself, but in his God.

"It is not in me: God shall give Pharaoh an answer of peace." (Genesis 41:16)

The Pivot

From Interpreter to Architect

Here is where most people miss the boat. Pharaoh tells Joseph the disturbing dream of the seven fat cows being devoured by the seven lean cows. Joseph interprets the dream: Seven years of abundance followed by seven years of famine.

If Joseph had stopped there, he would have been given a nice reward, perhaps a gold coin, and sent back to the dungeon—or maybe given a job as a court soothsayer. Why? Because **prophets identify problems, leaders design solutions.** Pharaoh didn't just need to know *what* was happening; he needed to know *what to do* about it. A diagnosis without a prescription is just bad news.

Joseph didn't just stop at the *spiritual* interpretation. He immediately, without being asked, pivoted to *strategic* application. He transitioned from the mystic to the manager in a single breath.

Business Continuity Planning (BCP)

What Joseph proposes here is a textbook **Business Continuity Plan**. In modern business terms, he performs a rapid SWOT analysis and proposes a comprehensive mitigation strategy. First, he conducts a risk assessment, identifying a "single point of failure" in the Egyptian economy, the dependence on the Nile's flooding cycle. He forecasts a black swan event: seven years of total economic collapse that would wipe out the empire.

Next, he offers a Mitigation Strategy: The "20% Reserve Requirement." He suggests a flat tax of one-fifth (20%) during the boom years to create a surplus. This is brilliant macroeconomics—high enough to build a massive reserve, but low enough (80% retention) to keep the populace motivated to produce. It balances austerity with incentive. It uses behavioral economics to save the nation. Finally, he outlines a governance structure, calling for a "discerning and wise man" (a CEO) and "officers" (middle management) to oversee the execution.

The Grain Silos

Archaeology confirms that grain was the currency of the Nile. The Middle Kingdom saw the rise of massive administrative centers and granaries. Joseph was proposing a massive civil engineering project that would require centralizing the entire economy of Egypt. This required knowledge of geometry (to build the silos), storage capacity (to hold seven years of food), pest control (to prevent rot), and logistics (distribution).

Where did he learn this? He likely gleaned it by observing Potiphar's estates and managing the prison's food supply. Every menial task in his past was a brick in the foundation of his future strategy. The prison roster taught him to manage the national census. Potiphar's pantry taught him to manage the national reserve.

The point is, maximizing the moment requires more than just intuition; it requires a plan. When your opportunity comes, don't just point out the issues. Don't just interpret the "vibe." Walk in with the solution in your hand. Be the architect of the future, not just the critic of the present.

The Theology of Readiness

Pharaoh is so impressed—not just by the interpretation, but by the *wisdom* of the plan—that he promotes Joseph on the spot. He gives him his signet ring, robes of linen, and a gold chain. And he renames him. He calls him *Zaphenath-Paneah* (or Safenat-Paneach).

The Name Change

Scholars have long debated this Egyptian title. A strong linguistic reconstruction suggests it comes from the Egyptian meaning "The God Speaks, and He Lives" or "The Revealer of Mysteries."

This is significant. Pharaoh wasn't just giving him a nickname; he was naturalizing him. In the Ancient Near East, a name change signified a change in destiny, ownership, and authority. By accepting this name, Joseph was stepping into a role where he would be the voice of God to the empire. He was the bridge between the Divine and the desperate. He became the conduit through which heaven invaded earth. He accepted the cultural rebranding to facilitate the spiritual mission.

This is the ultimate goal of the Christian professional. We are called to be "Revealers of Mysteries" in the marketplace. We are called to bring divine wisdom into secular problems. We are called to have solutions that the world cannot generate on its own because they come from the Spirit of Wisdom. We are called to walk into boardrooms, hospitals, and schools and provide the "God-breathed" solution that saves the day. But remember the order: You cannot reveal mysteries if you haven't spent time in the secret place with the Mystery Maker, and you cannot manage the grain of Egypt if you haven't been faithful with the bread in the prison.

Sovereignty and Responsibility

There is a beautiful tension here. God is sovereign. He gave the dreams. He orchestrated the famine. He softened Pharaoh's heart. But **Joseph** was responsible for the preparation. Joseph had to learn the language. Joseph had to stay bitter-free. Joseph had to shave. We work as if it all depends on us, and we pray as if it all depends on God. We pursue excellence as our worship, and we trust God for the promotion. We sharpen the axe, but we trust God to fell the tree.

My Reflection

My friend, do not despise the day of small beginnings. Do not curse the pit. Do not resent the prison. Do not look at the silence of your current season as the absence of God. It is the *presence* of preparation. You are being seasoned. You are being strengthened. You are being emptied of self so you can be filled with substance. The silence is not rejection; it is the hush of the lecture hall before the professor speaks.

The junior analyst mastering the data is not just an employee; he is a future CEO in training. The songwriter weeping over a melody in the basement is not wasting time; she is a future psalmist for the nations being forged in the fire. The mid-career professional studying late into the night is not foolish; he is a future pillar of the organization being constructed.

The call is coming. The "Pharaoh" of your industry—the person with the resources to fund your vision, the platform to amplify your voice, the authority to open the door—is going to have a dream they cannot interpret. They will wake up troubled. They will have a problem money cannot solve. They will have a crisis their consultants cannot fix. In that moment, they won't care about your pedigree, your marketing, your complaints, or your past.

They will call for someone who has the Spirit of God and the spirit of excellence. They will call for someone who has mastered the data and mastered their ego. They will call for someone who has been faithful in the dark.

Will you be ready? Will you be ready to shave? Will you be ready to change your clothes? Will you be ready to stand tall and offer the solution?

Get back to work. Your obscurity is your university. And graduation day is closer than you think.

Chapter Action Guide

1. The "Prison" Perspective Shift (Cognitive Reframing): Begin by identifying the one area of your life where you feel most stuck, hidden, or undervalued, whether that is an entry-level job, a small ministry, or a financial struggle. Then, reframe this area by renaming it "The Training Ground." Instead of asking "Why is this happening to me?", ask "What skill is this trying to teach me that I will need in my palace season?" Finally, act on this by listing three specific skills—technical or relational—you can extract from this painful situation this week.

2. The Thirty-Second Elevator Pitch (The "Pharaoh" Test) Imagine if the CEO or key decision-maker turned to you right now in an elevator and asked, "What is the one thing we should do differently to thrive next year?" Would you have an answer? Draft a three-sentence proposal for a solution to a problem your organization faces. First, state the problem (The Lean Cows). Second, propose the solution (The Grain Silos). Third, identify the first step (The Wise Man). Memorize this pitch so you are ready to deliver it with "shaved and changed" confidence.

3. The Strategic Pre-Mortem Fast forward five years in your mind. Imagine a crisis hits your industry or your family. What is the most likely cause? Determine what "grain"—resources, skills, emergency funds, relationships, spiritual depth—should you be storing up *now* to survive that famine? Create your 20% savings plan today.

4. The Spiritual Audit Read Psalm 105:17-19, which reminds us that *"Until the time that his word came to pass, the word of the Lord tested him."* Pray specifically: "Lord, help me to pass the test of the iron. Keep my heart soft while my skills become sharp. Do not promote me until I am ready to carry the weight of the glory."

If you are navigating a high-stakes transition and want to apply this framework to your own situation with clarity and discipline, scan the QR code below for a Transition Readiness Chat.

CHAPTER 10

The Unstoppable Version of You

"The unstoppable version of you is not revealed by opportunity—it is forged by the unseen disciplines that prepare you to survive it."

The Physiology of Destiny

There is a moment in every leader's life, a specific, terrifying, and exhilarating millisecond, where the private work of the soul intersects with the public needs of the world. We call this *Emergence*.

Most people fundamentally misunderstand the mechanics of success. They view it as an event, a lottery win, or a sudden promotion. They look at the "overnight successes" of Silicon Valley or the sudden platform of a viral influencer and assume that visibility is an accident of timing or the result of a single viral moment. They see the harvest, but they missed the planting, the watering, the weeding, and the long seasons of drought.

If you look closely at the architecture of human greatness, particularly through the lens of Scripture, archaeology, management theory, and modern psychology, you realize that true success isn't an event; it is a *state of being*. It is the unstoppable version of you finally catching up to the vision God placed in your spirit decades ago. It is the moment when your internal character density finally matches your external opportunity. Without that matching density, the external pressure of success will crush you. Emergence, therefore, is not about finding a spotlight; it is about becoming a person who can hold the weight of the light without burning out.

The Neuroscience of the "New You"

Psychologically, emergence triggers a violent battle in the brain. Your basal ganglia, the habit center, responsible for automated behaviors, craves the safety of the known, even if the known is painful. To emerge is to violate the brain's law of homeostasis. It requires what neuroscientists call *directed neuroplasticity*: the conscious, repeated decision to wire your brain for a future that hasn't happened yet. This is not passive hope; it is active neurological reconstruction.

When you step out of your comfort zone, your amygdala (the fear center) screams "Danger!" It perceives social visibility and high-stakes leadership as a threat to survival, akin to being chased by a predator. This biological resistance is why so many potential leaders self-sabotage right at the threshold of their breakthrough. They experience "identity lag," a cognitive dissonance where their internal self-concept as a slave, prisoner, or imposter has not yet caught up to their external reality as a prime minister, CEO, or leader. They are wearing the signet ring, but they still feel the shackles.

The gap between your current reality and your future identity is where the war is fought. **Tony Robbins** often notes that humans will always follow through on who they believe they *are*. Identity is the strongest force in the human personality. If you believe you are a victim, your Reticular Activating System (RAS)—the bundle of nerves at your brainstem that filters unnecessary information—will filter the world to find evidence of oppression. It will literally blind you to opportunity. It will delete success signals from your conscious awareness. If you believe you are a deliverer, your RAS will filter the world to find opportunities for contribution. It will highlight resources you previously ignored, turning invisible assets into visible tools.

Think of the story of Joseph in the book of Genesis. We love the ending, the prime minister of Egypt, the signet ring, the fine linen, the bowing brothers. We love the *palace.* But the palace was not where Joseph emerged. The palace was simply where he was announced. Joseph emerged in the dark. He emerged in the silence. He emerged when he decided that his geography would not dictate his psychology.

In the language of **Tony Robbins**, biography is not destiny. Your past does not equal your future unless you live there. In the language of **Peter Drucker**, the best way to predict the future is to create it. Joseph didn't wait for the future; he managed himself into it. This chapter is your blueprint for visibility. It is not for the faint of heart. It is for the believer who feels the pressure of a promise that hasn't happened yet.

The Disruption of Comfort

The Law of the Lid, Archaeology, and Crisis Management

"Now Israel loved Joseph more than any of his other sons... and he made him a coat of many colors." (Genesis 37:3)

Emergence always begins with a disruption. For Joseph, it was the coat—the *ketonet passim.* Theologically, this was a mantle of distinction. The Hebrew phrase implies a tunic with long sleeves, extending to the ankles. In a culture of shepherds and laborers who wore short tunics for ease of movement, a long-sleeved tunic was a functional statement that this boy did not work with his hands. He was in management. He was the designated successor, chosen over the firstborn.

Strategically, however, this was a personal branding disaster. Joseph had the vision, symbolized by his dreams of sheaves and stars, but he lacked the political intelligence. He announced his superiority to his brothers without understanding the complex stakeholder landscape of his own family. He shared his "Q4 projections" of dominance with the very people who stood to lose market share. He violated the first rule of power dynamics: never outshine the master, or in this case, the collective brotherhood, without a strategy. His naivety created a vacuum of envy that inevitably collapsed on top of him. He was a visionary without a container, a leader without a coalition.

And so, the pit.

The "pit" was likely a limestone cistern located near the trade route of Dothan. Archaeologists have excavated numerous bottle-shaped cisterns in this region, designed to hold water during the rainy season. However, in the dry season, they became muddy, suffocating cells—narrow at the top and widening at the bottom, making escape impossible without a rope. The walls would have been slick with algae and mud, damp and cold even in the heat of the day.

Joseph was trapped in the earth's silence, mere yards away from a bustling trade route. The contrast is devastating. He could hear the Ishmaelite caravan—the bells of the camels, the shouting of traders dealing in gum, balm, and myrrh. The world of global commerce was moving on just feet away, while he was stuck in the dark. This highlights the primary pain of the Pit: *The market moves on while you are stuck.* It creates a sense of irrelevance that cuts deeper than the physical confinement. The psychological torture of the Pit is the feeling that you have been deleted from history.

The Pivot

When you are in the Pit, you are in a **Turnaround Scenario**. Your "market value" has seemingly dropped to zero. You have been stripped of your assets, represented by the coat, and your network, represented by your family. The immature leader enters a state of *Learned Helplessness*, a psychological condition described by Martin Seligman where one believes that no amount of effort will change the outcome, leading to passivity and clinical depression. This is the danger zone where bitterness takes root.

The strategic leader, however, executes a **Pivot**. They realize that while they cannot control the macro-environment of the brothers, the cistern, or the slavery, they can control their micro-response. They shift from an external locus of control, believing "they did this to me," to an internal locus of control, asking "what can I create from this?" This is the moment where resilience is born—not as a feeling, but as a strategic decision. It is the refusal to accept the current data as the final conclusion.

Consider **Violet**.

Seven years ago, Violet was a cashier at a struggling retail chain. She held a degree in logistics but had been laid off during a corporate merger. She felt overqualified, invisible, and humiliated. The "Pit" for her was the monotony of the register and the rudeness of customers who treated her as part of the machinery.

Initially, Violet adopted a victim mindset. She told herself that she was a logistics expert and that this work was beneath her. She believed the system was rigged against her. In this phase, her work was sloppy, her attitude was resentful, and her energy was toxic. She was waiting for someone to rescue her, spending her breaks scrolling through LinkedIn and seething with jealousy at her former colleagues' promotions. She was digging the pit deeper with her own attitude.

Eventually, Violet realized no rescue was coming. She refused to die in the Pit. She adopted a **Blue Ocean Strategy** right at the register. She realized that the "Red Ocean" was the competitive corporate ladder she couldn't reach, but the "Blue Ocean" was the uncontested space of customer experience at Lane 4. She began to treat her register as a micro-business. She optimized the bagging process using her logistics background in operations management, grouping items by density and fragility to increase packing speed by 15%. She memorized the names and preferences of regular customers, effectively creating a "loyalty program" of personal connection. She reorganized the impulse-buy rack during downtime to maximize yield.

She didn't wait for the title of "manager." She led from the register. Six months later, a regional director noticed that her lane moved 20% faster than any other in the district and had the highest customer satisfaction scores. She had become indispensable. Today, Violet is the regional operations manager for the Northeast. She didn't emerge when she got the promotion; she emerged when she treated the Pit as a laboratory for excellence.

Managing Up

Joseph mastered the art of **Upward Management**. He earned Potiphar's trust so completely that Potiphar "did not know what he had saved for the bread which he ate." This is the ultimate goal of any executive assistant or operations manager: to create such a frictionless environment for the leader that they can focus entirely on their high-level function.

Joseph delivered **Operational Excellence**, embodying **Peter Drucker's** distinction: *Efficiency is doing things right; effectiveness is doing the right things.* Joseph did both. He managed assets he didn't own with better stewardship than the owner. He treated the slave quarters and the spreadsheets with the same level of integrity. He understood the **Principal-Agent Theory** instinctively—aligning his actions perfectly with the interests of the owner, eliminating the "agency cost" that usually plagues businesses.

How did he survive the drudgery and the trauma of slavery? He likely accessed what psychologist Mihaly Csikszentmihalyi calls *Flow*. By engaging fully in the complexity of managing the estate, Joseph transformed a slave's labor into an executive's challenge. He found "intrinsic motivation," doing it for the sake of excellence, rather than "extrinsic motivation," doing it for pay or freedom. This ability to find meaning in the mundane is the hallmark of resilient leaders. He refused to let his status as a slave dictate his standard as a leader. He understood that his work was an offering to God, not just a duty to Potiphar.

The Integrity Gap and Risk Management

The climax of this season is the encounter with Potiphar's wife. This was a **Risk Management** test. Visibility without integrity is a liability. The higher you rise, the more "Potiphar's Wives" will appear in the form of temptations, shortcuts, ethical compromises, or "easy money."

This temptation was not just sexual; it was political. Potiphar's wife was a path to power. Sleeping with her could have solidified his status or protected him from her wrath. She represented the "shortcut" to influence. Refusing her was a guaranteed path to destruction. Joseph chose destruction over corruption. He understood that a platform built on compromise will eventually collapse under the weight of the lie.

Take the case of Caspian, a tech founder whose first startup was a "unicorn" idea. He raised millions, bought the fast cars, and lived the "coat of many colors" life. But he lacked integrity in his code and his culture. He ignored bugs and operational debt to hit launch dates. He treated his team as expendable resources. The company collapsed under the weight of his ego and technical debt.

Caspian lost everything—his reputation, his capital, his confidence. He had to restart his career as a junior developer at a friend's stable, unexciting firm—his "Potiphar's House." It was a humbling demotion. Through this ego death, Caspian had to learn to code again, not as a rockstar, but as a craftsman. He focused on "corporate governance," beginning with personal self-governance. He refused to cut corners. He mentored younger developers without seeking credit. He documented his code meticulously, treating the work as sacred even though he wasn't the CEO.

Three years later, Caspian launched his second venture. This time, investors didn't just back the idea; they backed *Caspian*. They saw a man who had been humbled, who had proven he could be faithful with another man's code, and who was now "fireproof" against the arrogance that destroyed him before.

The Prison – The Incubation of Vision

Strategic Networking and The Stockdale Paradox

Joseph does the right thing and gets the wrong result. He is thrown into prison. This is the hardest phase of Emergence: the "delayed gratification" phase. It feels like a burial, but structurally, it is a planting. It is the dark night of the soul where the vision seems to die completely.

The Hebrew word for prison here, *Sohar*, is rare and implies a "Round House" or fortress. This wasn't a common jail for thieves; it was the king's prison, a holding tank for high-level political detainees like the royal butler and baker. These were men who had fallen out of favor with Pharaoh. Joseph was not just sitting in a cell; he was effectively in a "networking mixer" with the disgraced elite of Pharaoh's court. He was learning the protocols, the gossip, the diplomatic language, and the politics of the Palace from the inside. He was getting a PhD in Statecraft while sitting in a dungeon. He learned about the king's diet, the king's temper, and the king's anxieties from the men who served him daily.

The Management Insight: Weak Ties

Sociologist Mark Granovetter coined the term **"The Strength of Weak Ties."** Your closest friends, or strong ties, usually possess the same information and network that you do. Your acquaintances, or weak ties, like a former Butler, are the bridges to new worlds like the Palace.

Joseph didn't just interpret dreams; he engaged in **strategic alliances**. He solved a problem for the Butler, planting a seed of influence. He leveraged his spiritual gift to create value for a stakeholder who could eventually advocate for him. He understood that networking isn't about asking for favors; it's about depositing value. He sowed seeds in a season where he had no harvest. He served a man who could offer him nothing in the immediate moment, trusting in the compounding interest of kindness.

In prison, Joseph embodies what Jim Collins calls the **Stockdale Paradox**, named after Admiral James Stockdale, a prisoner of war in Vietnam. The paradox is this: *You must retain faith that you will prevail in the end, regardless of the difficulties, AND at the same time confront the most brutal facts of your current reality.* Joseph knew he would bow, as per his dream, but he confronted the reality of the prison discipline. He didn't just pray for release; he managed the prison. The warden gave him authority over the other prisoners. He was the "CEO of the Dungeon." He optimized the prison environment, likely improving sanitation, order, and morale. He bloomed where he was planted, even though the soil was toxic.

Consider **Rose**, who battled the "prison" of severe clinical depression and the loss of a child.

For five years, she felt abandoned by God. She was in the *Sohar* of grief, a round house of despair with no exit. During her darkest time, she engaged in powerful meaning-making. She started a support group for three other women grieving loss. She didn't have her own healing yet. She was "interpreting the dreams" of others while living in her own nightmare. She chose to serve despite her pain. She realized that her pain was a credential that allowed her to enter spaces of suffering others could not.

This is **Servant Leadership** weaponized, leading to **Post-Traumatic Growth**. As she poured out, she began to fill up. Today, Rose runs a national non-profit for grieving parents. Her authority doesn't come from a degree; it comes from the *scars*. When she speaks, people listen, because she has "prison cred." She emerged with a testimony that is bulletproof because it was forged in the fire.

If you are in a prison right now—a dead-end job, a health crisis, a financial hole—ask yourself the **Tony Robbins** question: *What is the empowering meaning you can give to this prison?* Is it a tomb, or is it a womb? The only difference is what you decide to birth while you are in the dark.

The Palace – The Platform of Purpose

Scenario Planning, Macroeconomics, and Change Management

"Now therefore, let Pharaoh select a discerning and wise man..." (Genesis 41:33)

The call comes. "Hastily." Emergence happens slowly, then suddenly. Joseph stands before Pharaoh. He interprets the dream. But then—and this is the key to unstoppability—he pivots. He stops being a prophet and starts being a **consultant**. He doesn't just give the diagnosis of seven years of famine; he gives the *prescription*. He moves from "Here is what God is saying" to "Here is what Egypt must do," transitioning from spiritual insight to structural implementation. This pivot is where most spiritual leaders fail—they can identify the problem, but they cannot architect the solution.

The Strategic Framework: Counter-Cyclical Economics

Joseph proposes the first recorded instance of **Keynesian Counter-Cyclical Economic Policy**. His approach was a masterclass in macroeconomic stability, unfolding in three distinct stages. First, he engaged in **Forecasting**, accepting the dream as a reliable fourteen-year market forecast. He identified the "Black Swan" event of the famine before it happened, acting as a true **Futurist** who looks beyond the immediate quarter to the long-term horizon.

Next, he proposed **Centralization**. He advised appointing a "discerning man" or CEO with centralized authority to override local inefficiencies and hoarding. He established a federal reserve of grain, nationalizing the food supply to prevent price gouging and starvation. He understood that a crisis requires a unified chain of command.

Finally, he mandated **Resource Allocation**. He imposed a 20% flat tax on grain during the boom years. In a time of abundance, the natural human tendency is to consume and expand. Joseph enforced **Savings**, creating a sovereign wealth fund of food for the bust years. This required immense political will—telling people to tighten their belts when the harvest is overflowing. It was a policy of unpopular prudence that saved the nation from inevitable collapse.

Historically, Joseph likely rose during the **Hyksos Period** (Second Intermediate Period), where Semitic "Shepherd Kings" ruled Lower Egypt. A native Egyptian Pharaoh might have despised a Hebrew shepherd, but a Hyksos ruler would have welcomed a fellow Semite with administrative genius. This reminds us that God controls the market conditions. He positioned Joseph in the exact century where his ethnicity would not be a barrier to his destiny. God's timing is not just spiritual; it is geopolitical.

Change Management (Kotter's Model)

Joseph executes **John Kotter's 8-Step Change Model** flawlessly. He began by creating urgency, framing the famine in a way that demanded immediate attention. He then built a coalition with Pharaoh and his court, securing executive sponsorship immediately. With this backing, he formed a strategic vision to "Store the grain" that was clear and communicable. He then enlisted a volunteer army, gathering corn "as the sand of the sea" and mobilizing the entire nation in a massive logistics operation. Finally, he generated short-term wins as the barns filled, reinforcing trust in the plan.

The Unstoppable You: Sustainability

Many leaders get the promotion and crash. Psychologists call this **"Success Depression"** or the "Arrival Fallacy." They reach the palace, but they lack the character to sustain the weight of the glory. They become narcissistic, paranoid, or burnt out. Joseph lasted eighty years.

He achieved this sustainability through **Systems Thinking**. He built **Supply Chain Redundancy** by placing storehouses in every city, not just the capital. He didn't rely on a single point of failure. This meant that even if one city's administration failed, the nation would survive.

He also exercised profound **Emotional Intelligence** by forgiving his brothers. The ultimate sign of the "Unstoppable Version of You" is how you handle those who hurt you. If Joseph used his power to destroy his brothers, he would have destroyed the workforce of the future nation of Israel and the lineage of the Messiah. Revenge is expensive; forgiveness is an investment.

Joseph said, *"You meant evil against me; but God meant it for good."* (Genesis 50:20). This is **Tony Robbins' "Reframing"** on a divine level. He reframed thirteen years of abuse as a strategic deployment by God to save the world. A bitter leader is a brittle leader. Forgiveness was not just a moral act; it was a **Strategic Preservation of Human Capital**. He realized that his brothers were not the villains of his story; they were the unwitting agents of his destiny. They pushed him to the place God needed him to be.

My Reflections

We have traversed the geography of Emergence. Now, you must execute the strategy based on your current location. You are likely in one of three stages, and each demands a specific directive.

If You Are in The Pit (Disruption)

Your strategy is to Pivot. You must interrupt the pattern of "Learned Helplessness" and refuse to be a victim or let the silence of the pit become the silence of your soul. Your key performance indicator is to commit to one act of service per day that adds value to someone else's metric, measuring your day not by how you feel, but by who you helped. Stop digging. Stop complaining about the coat you lost. Start branding yourself as a problem solver. If you are a cashier, be the best cashier in the district. If you are unemployed, be the best volunteer your church has ever seen. Master the micro.

If You Are in The Prison (Delay)

Your strategy is Upskilling & Networking. Practice "Active Waiting," understanding that this is not passive waiting but preparation, the athlete in the locker room before the game. Use this quarter to learn one new marketable skill, such as coding, finance, public speaking, or AI prompting. Add a tool to your belt that you didn't have when you entered the prison. Identify one "Butler," an influencer or connector you can serve without expectation of immediate return. Solve a problem for them. Be the solution to their headache. Pray that the Lord maximizes your capacity while you wait for your calling. Build bridges before you need to cross them.

If You Are in The Palace (Influence)

Your strategy is legacy & succession planning. Beware the "hedonic treadmill" and don't just consume your success. Realize that the palace is a platform for service, not a lounge for comfort.

Identify three "young Josephs" to mentor and pull them out of their pits. Invest in the generation that will replace you. Remember to store the grain. Build systems that will outlast you. Use your influence to protect the vulnerable. Ensure that your organization can survive without you.

You are not an accident. You are not a victim of the economy, your boss, or your upbringing. You are a deployable asset of the Kingdom of God. The world doesn't need more people who want the title; it needs people who have the *strategy* of the Palace and the *humility* of the Pit.

The version of you that is addicted to comfort must die so that the version of you that is addicted to purpose can live. The world is groaning, waiting for the sons and daughters of God to stop hiding in the cisterns and start managing the silos.

Step out of the shadows. Put on the garment of praise. Manage your state. Serve the people. Execute the plan. **Emerge.**

Strategic Audit

Before you close this chapter, conduct a personal strategic audit. Perform a **SWOT Analysis** to honestly assess your internal Strengths and Weaknesses, as well as the external Opportunities and Threats in your current "Pit" or "Prison." Take the **Potiphar Test**: Are you delivering operational excellence in a job you feel "overqualified" for? Are you trustworthy with the "inner chambers" of your boss's business? Engage in **Scenario Planning** by asking: If a "famine" (job loss, market crash, industry disruption) hit your sector in seven years, what "grain" should you be storing now in terms of savings, diversified skills, and deep relationships? Finally, conduct a **Forgiveness Audit**. Is there a "brother" or betrayer you are holding a grudge against? How is that grudge capping your leadership lid?

If you are navigating a high-stakes transition and want to apply this framework to your own situation with clarity and discipline, scan the QR code below for a Transition Readiness Chat.

Bibliography and Further Reading

Aling, Charles F. *Egypt and Bible History: From Earliest Times to 1000 B.C.* Grand Rapids, MI: Baker Book House, 1981.

Alter, Robert. *Genesis: Translation and Commentary.* New York: W.W. Norton & Company, 1996.

Bandura, Albert. *Self-Efficacy: The Exercise of Control.* New York: Freeman, 1997.

Blanchard, Ken. *Leading at a Higher Level: Blanchard on Leadership and Creating High-Performing Organizations.* Upper Saddle River, NJ: FT Press, 2018.

Blanchard, Ken, and Renee Broadwell, eds. *Servant Leadership in Action: How You Can Achieve Great Relationships and Results.* Oakland, CA: Berrett-Koehler Publishers, 2018.

Blanchard, Ken, and Phil Hodges. *Lead Like Jesus: Lessons from the Greatest Leadership Role Model of All Time.* Nashville: Thomas Nelson, 2005.

Blanchard, Ken, and Spencer Johnson. *The One Minute Manager.* New York: William Morrow, 1982.

British Museum. *Papyrus Chester Beatty III (The Dream Book).* London: British Museum.

The Brooklyn Papyrus (35.1446). Brooklyn Museum, Middle Kingdom Collection.

Collins, Jim. *Good to Great: Why Some Companies Make the Leap... and Others Don't.* New York: Harper Business, 2001.

Csikszentmihalyi, Mihaly. *Flow: The Psychology of Optimal Experience.* New York: Harper & Row, 1990.

David, A. Rosalie. *The Pyramid Builders of Ancient Egypt: A Modern Investigation of Pharaoh's Workforce.* London: Routledge, 1986.

De Botton, Alain. *Status Anxiety.* New York: Pantheon, 2004.

Doidge, Norman. *The Brain That Changes Itself: Stories of Personal Triumph from the Frontiers of Brain Science.* New York: Viking, 2007.

Drucker, Peter F. *The Effective Executive: The Definitive Guide to Getting the Right Things Done.* New York: Harper Business.

Duhigg, Charles. *The Power of Habit: Why We Do What We Do in Life and Business.* New York: Random House, 2012.

Dweck, Carol S. *Mindset: The New Psychology of Success.* New York: Random House, 2006.

Eagleman, David. *Incognito: The Secret Lives of the Brain.* New York: Pantheon, 2011.

Edmondson, Amy C. *The Fearless Organization: Creating Psychological Safety in the Workplace.* Hoboken, NJ: Wiley, 2018.

Eisenberger, Naomi I., Matthew D. Lieberman, and Kipling D. Williams. "Does Rejection Hurt? An fMRI Study of Social Exclusion." *Science* 302, no. 5643 (2003): 290–292.

Ericsson, Anders, and Robert Pool. *Peak: Secrets from the New Science of Expertise.* Boston: Houghton Mifflin Harcourt, 2016.

Erikson, Erik H. *Identity: Youth and Crisis.* New York: W.W. Norton, 1968.

Festinger, Leon. *A Theory of Cognitive Dissonance*. Stanford, CA: Stanford University Press, 1957.

Frankl, Viktor E. *Man's Search for Meaning*. Boston: Beacon Press, 1946.

Gallagher, Leigh. *The Airbnb Story*. Boston: Houghton Mifflin Harcourt, 2017.

Girard, René. *The Scapegoat*. Baltimore: Johns Hopkins University Press.

Goleman, Daniel. *Emotional Intelligence: Why It Can Matter More Than IQ*. New York: Bantam Books, 1995.

Granovetter, Mark S. "The Strength of Weak Ties." *American Journal of Sociology* 78, no. 6 (1973): 1360–1380.

Hamilton, Victor P. *The Book of Genesis, Chapters 18–50*. Grand Rapids, MI: Eerdmans, 1995.

Handy, Charles. *The Empty Raincoat: Making Sense of the Future*. London: Arrow Books, 1994.

Heifetz, Ronald A. *Leadership Without Easy Answers*. Cambridge, MA: Belknap Press, 1994.

Heifetz, Ronald A., and Marty Linsky. *Leadership on the Line: Staying Alive Through the Dangers of Leading*. Boston: Harvard Business Review Press, 2002.

Herodotus. *The Histories, Book II*. Translated by Aubrey de Sélincourt. London: Penguin Classics.

Hoffmeier, James K. *Israel in Egypt: The Evidence for the Authenticity of the Exodus Tradition*. New York: Oxford University Press, 1996.

The Holy Bible. English Standard Version (ESV). Wheaton, IL: Crossway, 2001.

The Holy Bible. King James Version (KJV). Oxford: Oxford University Press.

The Holy Bible. New International Version (NIV). Grand Rapids, MI: Zondervan.

Isaacson, Walter. *Steve Jobs.* New York: Simon & Schuster, 2011.

Janoff-Bulman, Ronnie. *Shattered Assumptions: Toward a New Psychology of Trauma.* New York: Free Press.

Kass, Leon R. *The Beginning of Wisdom: Reading Genesis.* Chicago: University of Chicago Press, 2003.

Kaufman, Scott B., and Carolyn Gregoire. *Wired to Create: Unraveling the Mysteries of the Creative Mind.* New York: Perigee, 2015.

Kim, W. Chan, and Renée Mauborgne. *Blue Ocean Strategy.* Boston: Harvard Business Review Press.

Kitchen, Kenneth A. *On the Reliability of the Old Testament.* Grand Rapids, MI: Eerdmans, 2003.

Kotter, John P. *Leading Change.* Boston: Harvard Business Review Press.

Mandela, Nelson. *Long Walk to Freedom.* Boston: Little, Brown and Company, 1994.

Marcia, James E. "Development and Validation of Ego-Identity Status." *Journal of Personality and Social Psychology* 3, no. 5 (1966): 551–558.

Maslow, Abraham H. "A Theory of Human Motivation." *Psychological Review* 50, no. 4 (1943): 370–396.

Maxwell, John C. *Developing the Leader Within You 2.0.* Nashville: HarperCollins Leadership, 2018.

Maxwell, John C. *The 5 Levels of Leadership: Proven Steps to Maximize Your Potential.* New York: Center Street, 2011.

Maxwell, John C. *The 21 Irrefutable Laws of Leadership: Follow Them and People Will Follow You*. Nashville: Thomas Nelson, 2007.

Morris, Henry. *The Genesis Record: A Scientific and Devotional Commentary on the Book of Beginnings*. Grand Rapids, MI: Baker Books, 1976.

Patterson, Orlando. *Slavery and Social Death: A Comparative Study*. Cambridge, MA: Harvard University Press, 1982.

Peters, Tom, and Robert H. Waterman Jr. *In Search of Excellence: Lessons from America's Best-Run Companies*. New York: Harper & Row, 1982.

Ries, Eric. *The Lean Startup: How Today's Entrepreneurs Use Continuous Innovation to Create Radically Successful Businesses*. New York: Crown Business, 2011.

Robbins, Tony. *Awaken the Giant Within: How to Take Immediate Control of Your Mental, Emotional, Physical and Financial Destiny*. New York: Simon & Schuster, 1991.

Rotter, Julian B. "Generalized Expectancies for Internal Versus External Control of Reinforcement." *Psychological Monographs* 80, no. 1 (1966): 1–28.

Sarna, Nahum M. *The JPS Torah Commentary: Genesis*. Philadelphia: Jewish Publication Society, 1989.

Schlentz, Matthew. "Steve Jobs's 'Wilderness Years': The NeXT and Pixar Story." Stanford Graduate School of Business Case Study, 2011.

Scott, Kim. *Radical Candor: Be a Kick-Ass Boss Without Losing Your Humanity*. New York: St. Martin's Press, 2017.

Seligman, Martin E. P. "Learned Helplessness." *Annual Review of Medicine* 23 (1972): 407–412.

Seligman, Martin E. P. *Learned Optimism: How to Change Your Mind and Your Life.* New York: Knopf, 1991.

Taleb, Nassim Nicholas. *Antifragile: Things That Gain from Disorder.* New York: Random House, 2012.

Tedeschi, Richard G., and Lawrence G. Calhoun. "Posttraumatic Growth: Conceptual Foundations and Empirical Evidence." *Psychological Inquiry* 15, no. 1 (2004): 1–18.

Turner, Victor. *The Ritual Process: Structure and Anti-Structure.* Chicago: Aldine Transaction, 1969.

Voss, Chris. *Never Split the Difference: Negotiating as If Your Life Depended on It.* New York: Harper Business, 2016.

Walton, John H., Victor H. Matthews, and Mark W. Chavalas. *The IVP Bible Background Commentary: Old Testament.* Downers Grove, IL: InterVarsity Press, 2000.

Wilkinson, Toby. *The Rise and Fall of Ancient Egypt.* New York: Random House, 2010.

www.ingramcontent.com/pod-product-compliance
Lightning Source LLC
LaVergne TN
LVHW090517110826
845146LV00003B/893

* 9 7 9 8 9 0 4 1 7 2 1 2 1 *